I want my poetry to... volume 4

the conscious poets
inspired by . . . Monte Smith

Inner Child Press, ltd.

'building bridges of cultural understanding'

Credits

Authorship
The Conscious Poets

Foreword
Kimberly Burnham, Ph.D.

Preface
William S. Peters, Sr.

Cover Design
Inner Child Press International

In order to maintain each poet's authentic voice, this volume has not undergone the scrutiny of editing. Please take time to indulge each contributor for their own creativity and aspirations to convey their uniqueness.

hülya n. yılmaz, Ph.D.

Director of Editing ~
Inner Child Press International

General Information

I want my poetry to . . .
Volume 4

The Conscious Poets

1st Edition: 2025

This publishing is protected under Copyright Law as a "Collection". All rights for all submissions are retained by the individual author and/or artist. No part of this publishing may be reproduced, transferred in any manner without the prior WRITTEN CONSENT of the "Material Owner" or its representative, Inner Child Press. Any such violation infringes upon the creative and intellectual property of the owner pursuant to international and federal copyright law. Any queries pertaining to this "Collection" should be addressed to publisher of record.

Publisher Information:

Inner Child Press
intouch@innerchildpress.com
www.innerchildpress.com

This Collection is protected under U.S. and International Copyright Laws

Copyright © 2025: Inner Child Press

ISBN-13: 978-1-961498-53-2 (inner child press, ltd.)

$ 24.95

Poets, Writers . . . know that we are the enchanting magicians who nourish the seeds of dreams and thoughts . . . our words entice the hearts and minds of others to believe there is something grand about the possibilities that life has to offer, and our words tease it forth into action . . . for you are the Poet, the Writer to whom the Gift of Words has been entrusted . . .

~ wsp

Dedication

This volume is dedicated to

The poets of the world

Their vision...

Their consciousness...

Their message...

Poets . . .
sowing seeds in the
Conscious Garden of Life,
that those who have yet to come
may enjoy the Flowers.

Table of Contents

Preface — xi

I Want my poetry to . . .

Nolcha Fox	3
Til Kumari Sharma	5
Robert Allen Goodrich Valderrama	7
Timothy Payton	9
Carolyn Jones	11
Neha Bhandarkar	13
Zan V. Johns	16
Agnishikha Bhatt	18
Alexandra Nicod	20
Alexander José Villarroel Salazar	22
Chyrel J. Jackson	25
Dušan Stojković	27
Yasmin S Brown	29
Caroline Nazareno Gabis	31
Dr. Brajesh Kumar Gupta	33
Tajalla Qureshi	35
Abeera Mirza	37
Sotirios A. Christopoulos	39
Errol D. Bean	41
Hannie Rouweler	44
Tamikio L. Dooley	46
Ivan Pozzoni	48
Huniie Parker	50

Table of Contents ...continued

Marcelo Sánchez	52
Shoshana Vegh	54
Akleema Ali	56
Hussein Habasch	58
Lilla Latus	60
Gordana Sarić	62
Swayam Prashant	64
Poul Lynggaard Damgaard	66
Smruti Ranjan Mohanty	68
Ifeanyi Enoch Onuoha	71
Marlon Salem Gruezo	73
Dr. Biswas	75
Marion de Vos-Hoekstra	77
Ibrahim Honjo	79
Tyran Prizren Spahiu	82
Ngozi Olivia Osuoha	84
Aleksandra Sołtysiak	86
Rahim Karim (Karimov)	88
Tống Thu Ngân	90
Izabela Zubko	92
Mark Andrew Heathcote	94
Tanja Ajtic	97
Noreen Ann Snyder	99
Aziz Mountassir	102
Irena Jovanović	104
Naheed Akhtar	106
Gail Weston Shazor	108

Table of Contents ... continued

Gregoire Marshall	110
Nour elhouda Guerbaz	113
Mohamed Abdel Aziz Shameis	115
Nandita De nee Chatterjee	117
Kimberly Burnham	120
Teodozja Świderska	122
Anna Maria Stępień	124
Sujata Paul	126
Kay Salady	128
Mark Fleisher	130
Md Ejaj Ahamed	132
Celia Kurdab Hamadeh	134
Jill Delbridge	136
Andy Kouroupos	139
Carthornia Kouroupos	141
Mutawaf Shaheed	143
Shareef Abdur Rasheed	145
hülya n. yılmaz	147
William S. Peters, Sr.	150

Epilogue

About Inner Child Press	156
Other Meaningful Anthologies	157

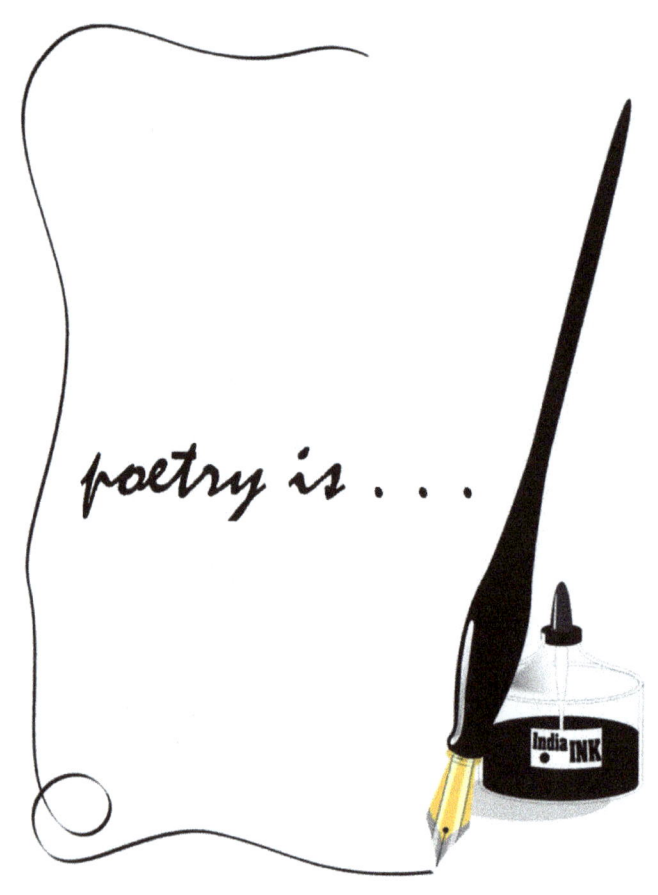

poetry is . . .

Poetry succeeds where instruction fails.

~ wsp

. . .
x

Preface

I want my poetry to . . .

Why do we write? . . . What do you want your poetry to do?

Back in 2012, on Jill Delbridge's poetry radio show, The Artists Lounge, we, the poetry community were challenged by poet/activist Monte Smith to examine our purpose as poets. Our purpose for writing our verse is perhaps a very personal reaction of who we are, but truth be told, we have voices that can be at times lent to effectuate change for the better by raising the consciousness of the heart of humanity.

We CAN move mountains if we but try.

We can stimulate the hearts, minds and spirits of others through our poetic evocations .... what do you want your poetry to do?

In the following pages, you the reader will have an opportunity to peek behind the veil and perhaps arrive at an understanding of why, we poets do what we do. I hope you enjoy.

Bless up

Bill

Advisory Board

World Healing, World Peace Foundation
human beings for humanity

2025

worldhealingworldpeacefoundation.org

I want my poetry to... *volume* 4

the conscious poets
inspired by . . . Monte Smith

I want my poetry to . . . Volume 4

I want my poetry to... Volume 4
Nolcha Fox

Nolcha Fox's poems have been curated in print and online journals. Her poetry books are available on Amazon and Dancing Girl Press. Nominee for 2023 and 2025 Best of The Net, 2024 Best of the Net Anthology. Nominee for 2023 and 2024 Pushcart Prize. Editor of Chewers by Masticadores.

Website: https://writingaddiction2.wordpress.com/ and
https://nolchafox2.wixsite.com/nolcha-s-written-wor/blog
LinkedIn: https://www.linkedin.com/in/nolchafox/
Facebook: https://www.facebook.com/nolcha.fox/

I Want My Poetry to …

I want my poetry to
be the roses crying
red petals on the coffin.

I want my poetry to
be the stillness of the deer
framed by fog and birdsong.

I want my poetry to
be the geese flying
across my windshield.

I want my poetry to
be the captive inhale,
the moment before wonder escapes.

I want my poetry to . . . Volume 4
Til Kumari Sharma

Ms.Til Kumari Sharma is a Multi Award Winner in area from Paiyun 7- Hile Parbat, Nepal. Her writings are published in many countries. She is a featured-poet and best-selling co-author too. She is a poet and co-organizer of the World Record Book " HYPERPOEM". She is one of many artists to break a participant record to write a poem about the Eiffel Tower of France. She is made as "Poetic Legend of Asia" by Nigerian Painter.

I Want My Poetry to . . .

I like my verse to lead the earth.
Yes, really poem is the supreme queen of purity.
Creative and innovative worth is there.
So we can change the world of violence into peace through poetry.
Only blessing soul can draw poetic words originally.
Verse of higher mind can lead the universe alone with ethics.
We may take journey of the universe through the poetic words.
Poetic building is huge source of highest mind.
Respect poetic leading of the earth.
Poetry is the president of the literature.
It is the supreme leader to change the world with concept of the humanity.
The storm can be changed in fresh air by poetic formation.
The nation will be pure with poetic art.
Poem is the wise fellow to teach us the super wit.
So we can take flight in the earth without block of others when poem walks with our creativity.
Poetry is poet's monument to make alive forever.
The supreme leader of undead ethics is poetic art which never is in ditch.
Even sea waves can not break this monument.
Earthquake can not touch this poetic statue.
The fire can not touch the verse of originality of mine.
So I say that poetry is the strongest fighter or the hero of the earth.
I desire my poetry to be so as above lines mention.
We may move the war in peace if poetry leads the earth.

I want my poetry to . . . Volume 4
Robert Allen Goodrich Valderrama

Robert Allen Goodrich Valderrama (Panamá 1980): Poeta, writer creator of the blog My world www.robert-mimundo.blogspot.com and the creator of the Group in Facebook Amor por las Letras. Finalist for the Reinaldo Arenas Literary Prize Novel Version 2024, III Place Literary Contest Poetry as a livelihood - Cultural la Rueca and Marinka Foundation, Argentina 2024, Finalist of the Reinaldo Arenas Literary Prize Version Poetry 2017, intercontinental Prize for the Arts Dr. Maria Espinosa Peña-CCI Universal Poetic Utopia 2024, Letter from Texas Senator Ted Cruz-Washington DC 2024, Dr. Aziz Mountassir-CCI International Peace Prize Universal Poetic Utopia 2024, and others. His books are published in Lulu.com, Amazon and others.

I Want My Poetry to . . .

I want my to poetry to give a message of peace
of message of love and passion for the life.

I want to offer to you my verses
to give a message of peace and love for the entire world.

I am not a poet,
I am ambassador of peace with a pen.

I want to poetry to give a message of peace and love
for the entire world.

Do it with me
we can change the world
we can end the war
we can be the ambassador of peace with our pen.

I want my poetry to . . . Volume 4
Timothy Payton

Timothy Payton is a Writer, Abstract Artist, Spoken Word Artist, Recovery Coach Professional, Ambassador of Peace representing Ghana, West Africa and Universal Ambassador representing France, Self-Published Author and Best-selling Co-Author. Timothy is mostly known for his word art and elusive spoken word. Timothy also has a poetry book available on Amazon called "Scattered Colors".

I Want My Poetry to . . .

I want my poetry to...
Uplift and inspire,
Using my God given talent, to motivate & transpire.

I want my poetry to...
Put a voice within words,
To be heard within the heart and those lost to observe.

I want my poetry to...
Flow lively, full of life like blood,
Traveling within thoughts, into the atmosphere with Love.

I want my poetry to...
Be spread with blessed messages, weaving words into art,
Creating sweet emotions that are colorful throughout.

This was God's plan and wasn't mine,
It was placed within my DNA so carefully and divine.

I Want my poetry to...
Become like second nature and language as a labor of Love,
To create something intangible, yet, touches and holds you like a hug.

I want my poetry to...
Play a part in seeing a change,
A change for a better world of positive reinforcements and gains.

I want my poetry to...
Create words that hold massive power,
That can build up hope and bridges, into emotions and thoughts that were devoured.

I want my poetry to...
Be expressed universally, yet from a personal place,
For you to see yourself within words, like a reflection upon your face.

This was God's plan and wasn't mine,
It was placed within my DNA so carefully and divine.

I want my poetry to . . . Volume 4

Carolyn Jones

Carolyn Jones is a writer, educator, and bereavement chaplain licensed by the New York State Chaplain Task Force (NYSCTF). She is also a dedicated holistic health practitioner, holding certifications in herbalism, aromatherapy, reflexology, flower essence therapy, and acupuncture detoxification. Carolyn has authored <u>Incantations</u>, an affirmation guidebook and <u>Pick Up Your Bed and Walk: A Self-Care Guide to Improved Health</u>, a practical resource for individuals pursuing a healthier lifestyle. Her favorite literary genre is poetry, reflecting her deep passion for creative expression.

I Want My Poetry to . . .

I want my poetry to…
Rupture the amniotic sac that holds captive
self-evident truth.
Make invisible the distortions that infect innocent youth.
Flood the Earth with dialogue sprung from ancestral
knowing.
Guide souls to honor acts sacred…
The coming, the going.
Expose festering secrets in bowels of generational caverns.
Lay bare the wrongs exacted by perverse family patterns.
Document the sanctimonious chants of power-driven
gargoyles.
Snatch babies from a soup of venomous spoils.
Legalize the ringing of freedom all over the land.
Explain democracy in a way the dense understand.
Celebrate prevailing in spite of insults and lies.
Cauterize social hemorrhages, open closed eyes.
Navigate the living, raise the dead.
I can do that with poetry, yes, that's what I said…
My poetry can heal the sick and denounce a king.
It can make you laugh and call a thing a thing.
Obstruct unjust obstructions, peeling skin off
deceit.
Emerge from the shadows, once the task is complete.
In the face of disaster and unfathomable strife,
My words unite families and regenerate life.
Weaving syncopated sonnets,
I bind your mind to my soul.
Incubating our love, we emerge from the cold.
Mugwort blanket, archangel brigades,
Summon heavenly help and seraphic parades.
Conjuring instructions for trusting surrender,
Bathing in laughter and auric glow splendor.
Bless-ed be me for cherishing shards,
Born into redemption, Life shuffled the cards.
Stony the path, time always in motion,
My eyes on the skies, I sip bitters and potions.
When my guts spill in public, I atone with a kiss.
My Muse is my magic, my thoughts are my bliss.
I want my poetry to bear witness to this.

I want my poetry to... Volume 4
Neha Bhandarkar

Neha Bhandarkar is widely published Iconic trilingual author in Marathi, Hindi and English languages. She is published author of 16 books in 3 languages. She is also a genuine translator. Her poems have been translated into more than 15 inter- national languages and published in many countries. She embellished with numerous national and international awards for her consummate literary skill. She has bagged Hindi State Sahithya Academy Award twice, from Government of India. Her articles are included in syllabus of Amravati University of India.

I Want My Poetry to . . .

I want my poetry
To rise, not to set.

'O' dearest Poem!
Please do commit
To the poets around the world
That never will you die out
'Coz if you wane, so do the poets

Have you seen the sun fearful
Or the moon finished?

O dear Poem!
In the circumstantial dark and glow
Countless efforts would be made
To annihilate you
Even so, you rise again and again
As the sun and the moon
With a new ray of hope every time

Like a sweet cuckoo
Recognize the onset of spring
Affix the fragments of time
With the cultured civilizations
And enthrone the hearts of every one

Be as aromatic as the blue lotus
Be as fragrant as
the essence of musk
Keep waving your stole
With this blossoming land

Shower your pitter-patter
As the writing flow of poets
Gush relentlessly drifted away as a river
And keep sailing wantonly
On the word-ferry

I want my poetry to . . . Volume 4

I know it is not easy
To keep safe your existence
In the ocean-like Word-web
Even so, you try
Try to rise never to set

It is said,
"The world rests on
Endurance and hope".

I really want my poetry
To rise, not to set.

I want my poetry to . . . Volume 4
Zan V. Johns

Zan V. Johns is a world class author of three poetry collections and *What Matters Journal*. She has co-authored four international bestselling collaborative books and co-edited three poetry anthologies. Johns is the Women Speakers Association Poet Laureate and an editor of *Fine Lines Journal*. She is also an administrator for the Passion of Poetry. Her expressions appear in nearly one-hundred literary publications. Johns resides in Colorado, USA. ZanExpressions.com

I Want My Poetry to . . . Shine

I want my poetry to brightly shine
I touch the world line by line
I want my poetry to be a ray of sun
My lyrics will encourage everyone
My words of wisdom will help you cope
My vulnerability will offer hope
I'll extend the grace afforded to me
I want to comfort and set you free

My poetry will meet you wherever you are
It will lead you to your own North Star
I want to honor and make you proud
To make you smile or laugh out loud
To prompt your action with focused goals
To help you sort your unique role

I want my poetry to be an invitation
For silent voices to gain appreciation
My poetry greets you with open arms
Approving words add special charm
I want my poetry to be a salve—
A reminder to value what you have

I want my poetry to be a soft landing
To promote dialogue and understanding
I want my lyrics to share nothing but truth
To remove shadows beneath your roof
I want my poetry to be a peaceful stroll
To be the stream that ever flows
My lines will share occasional humor
Clarity and ease will squash the rumors

I want my poetry to shine shine shine
There will be light between the lines
You will feel valued—heard and seen
Verses will spark your dormant dreams
My expressions are undeniably clever
I want my poetry to last forever

I want my poetry to . . . Volume 4
Agnishikha Bhatt

Agnishikha Bhatt is an Indian doctor by profession. Having lived with the name tag of the land of my forefathers which I visited thrice as a tourist. My valley doesn't remember me it seems, yet i am hopeful of a good day when I am no longer a tourist there.

I Want My Poetry to . . . Exodus

I want my poetry to
send me back to my home.
Laughing on my exodus,
glad you may be.
Lost are the glens and glades,
misty vales, green hills,
no home to remember ,
as you burnt mine.
My dreams of cool breeze, flowers,
soaring heart in the land,
your deeds didn't stop,
turning salty drops into blood.
Rebuilding of my home in this life,
your eyes will see,
laughing on my exodus,
glad you may not be.

I want my poetry to... Volume 4
Alexandra Nicod

Alexandra Nicod is a multifaceted artist and poet, member of the Spanish General Society of Authors and Publishers, the Spanish Collegiate Association of Writers and the Spanish Actors Union.

I Want My Poetry to . . .

I want my poetry to be a crystal-clear river capable of washing away all the pain that your heart has accumulated since you were born, to become your Naiad and for the vowels I whisper in your ear to be the honey that covers your wounds and the consonants a million golden threads that sew your cuts so that they look bright and proud, showing the world the value of the survivor.

I want my poetry to be the life-giving breeze that cleanses every cell of your body of the atrocities committed against your people, to transform myself into your Sylph and for every breath of air that I create to move like a magical whirlwind purifying starry corners of this and other lives, of this and other generations of yours.

I want my poetry to be the hardest and most powerful rock of all time so that you can rest your sorrow on its slope, to metamorphose into your Cybele and to sing you the lullabies of your mother that you have not seen again.

I want my poetry to be the storm that breaks with the tyranny that has subjugated your tribe, to grow myself into Tempestas and invoke lightning bolts of justice and thunder of peace.

I want my poetry to be the moon that plays hide and seek with your dreams, to blend myself into Selene so that each shooting star brings a smile to your face and takes you through a time tunnel to the happy memories of your childhood.

I want my poetry to be the sun that you searched for in vain for so many years. The sun that had to hide behind clouds of social prohibitions, for me to be your Eos and your Hemera.

But above all, my love, I want my poetry to be ours, yours and mine, and to become the song of freedom, the love of the just and the homeland for the exiled. May your hand and mine never have to let go of each other again. May your gaze and mine look at the same horizon for all times to come. May your heart and mine rest together… in peace.

I want my poetry to . . . Volume 4

Alexander José Villarroel Salazar

Soy Alexander José Villarroel Salazar, 48 años, casado con 3 hijos. Soy de Venezuela, soy pastor, TSU en teología, matemático investigador en teoría de números, articulista en revistas científicas de matemáticas con 9 artículos publicados entre Venezuela, Ecuador y Costa Rica. Tengo dos solicitudes para ampliar dos artículos de editoriales de España y Moldavia para llevarlos a libros. Actualmente tengo varios artículos en revisión en revistas de Argentina, Colombia, México, Chile y España. Mis trabajos poseen teorías propias, novedosas, generadas a partir de estudios autodidactas y el uso del pensamiento divergente en temas diversos. Estoy en capacidad de enviarte artículos de ser necesario. Quiero que mis aportes sean reconocidos mundialmente. […]

Alexander José Villarroel Salazar
País: Venezuela

Quiero Que Mis Poemas

Quiero que mis poemas
Puedan brindar orientación
Para salir de los dilemas
Cual una buena explicación
Que traten acerca de temas
Que hay en el diario vivir
Y que cambien los sistemas
Que hay de actuar y de sentir.
Que sirvan como una guía
Como planes para avanzar
Y que sirvan día a día
Para a muchos motivar,
Es decir que mi poesía
No sea hablar por solo hablar
Sino que transmita armonía
Y anime muchos a cambiar
A salir de los pensamientos
Cargados de debilidad
Y que sirvan como un aliento
Para adquirir seguridad
Y que generen sentimientos
Para poder ser mejores
Y asi salir de los tormentos,
Los miedos y sinsabores,
Mostrando que cada persona
Tiene dones y valores
Y que Dios los galardona
Para vencer objeciones,
Para salir de lamentos
De miedos y de aflicciones
Y tener mejores momentos
Y adquirir más buenas condiciones.
Que Dios no quiere tus miedos
Que hoy impiden tu armonía
Que salgas de tus "No puedo"
De tus penas y agonías
Y que logres nuevas metas

I want my poetry to... Volume 4

Trabajando con empeño
Y que de forma completa
Se pueden cumplir tus sueños.
Quiero que todos mis escritos
Incidan positivamente
Y de un modo infinito
Produzca cambios realmente
Que anime a quien pueda leer
Para actuar prósperamente
Y que así puedan obtener
Una existencia diferente.

I want my poetry to . . . Volume 4
Chyrel J. Jackson

Chyrel J. Jackson is an International critically acclaimed poet and literary supernova. She is also a #1 Ranked Best Selling Amazon Author. Reared and raised in the South Suburbs outside Chicago. Black Literature influenced her writing. Chyrel Jackson writes in the spirit of her past great Literary ancestors.

Previously published works: SistersRoc'N'Rhyme Presents Poems in the Key of Life, Mirrored Images and Different Sides of the Same Coin Her writings: appear in multiple poetry Anthologies, Literary Journals, and International Global Magazines.

I Want My Poetry to…

I want my poetry to light
an inquisitive fire in younger
and future generations.
I want the words that are
written by me to inspire and
uplift every hurting unhealed
nation.
May the words I have lived
breathe life into weary lonely
unrested spirits.
With each new day comes
mercy and joy if only we are
brave enough to believe it.
I want the words that I write
to be a mirror that casts back
your own self-reflection.
I want my poetry to be the
hope that infuses and sparks
younger generations.
I want my words to be a home
for those who feel unsheltered.
I want your life to know that it
has value and promise.
Your personhood matters.
Finding myself within the pages of
a book made my soul fly.
Langston, Maya, Ntzoke, Sonia, and
Nikki set my Black soul on fire.
I speak life into you and release
my words into the universe.
May they set you free and help
you to break free from every
binding generational curse.
May the words that I have
lived breathe life into weary
restless unrested spirits.
With each new day comes
mercy and joy if only we are
brave enough to first live and be it.

I want my poetry to . . . Volume 4

Dušan Stojković

Dušan Stojković is a poet from Serbia, born on June 27, 1994. He published the collection of poetry „You are not cursed – it went in, it came out"(2021) and the poetry collection „Regret – You irrevocably left the fields" (2023).

His poem Cloud in Pants has been translated into 8 languages, and his poem „The natural course of things" into 11 languages.

Together with Jelena Sarić Cvetković, he is the founder of the MUK Association (Young Artists of Culture), he is the deputy president of the MUK Association and the general director of the international chamber of writers and artists CIESART for Serbia.

I Want My Poetry to . . .

I want my poetry to be
rain and wind and sun.
I want my poetry to be
orange and apple and
pomegranate.

A small house and a big yard.
Flowers in the garden and the
fence around the garden.

I want my poetry to be your home.

I want my poetry to . . . Volume 4

Yasmin S Brown

Yasmin S Brown is an international bestselling co-author, poet, author, and certified life coach. She owns Power Her Forward Ltd, an organization that utilizes literacy and coaching to help women move forward after adversity.

Yasmin S Brown has featured poetry in A Brave and Safe Space, The Talk, Myths and Legends an Extraordinary Collection, Cadence, Hush Life After Abuse, and many more. Brown finds poetic inspiration through life, emotion, and nature.

Yasmin S Brown's social media handles are Instagram and Facebook @yiryelements or visit her website for goods and services at https://www.yiry-elements.com.

I Want My Poetry to….

I want my poetry too,
flow with words of compassion,
A point of light with rhythmic wisdom,
swaying with heartfelt meaning.

I want my words to go deep into your soul,
to motivate an emotional response,
like an architect of words,
designing with care,
inspired by the Northern Lights.

Sending colorful sparks,
in an exuberant positive glow,
I want every line to shine,
connecting in memorable occasions.

I want to teach each verse,
with unity and understanding,
uplifting spirits, opening doors,
and replenishing your spirit with powerful delight.

I want my poetry to . . . Volume 4

Caroline Nazareno Gabis

Caroline 'Ceri Naz' Nazareno-Gabis, author of Velvet Passions of Calibrated Quarks, World Poetry Canada International Director to Philippines is a multi-awarded poet, editor, journalist, educator, peace and women's advocate. She believes that learning other's language and culture is a doorway to wisdom.

I Want My Poetry to . . .
Aurora, my poetry

I want my poetry to
stay like vapors of hope,
in every nation's vision
and pulses for lifetime flame;
I want my poetry to
become budding flowers,
in the dawn's name,
mirroring the aurora borealis
that spark smiles.

I want my poetry to
be running waters,
in dry seasons
to spill on your mouth
and moisten your throat
so you can read my poetry aloud.
I want my poetry to rhyme
in the aroma of black coffee
matched in the crispiness
of black sesame bread sticks
while we cherish
poets and the poetry magic.

I want my poetry to . . . Volume 4

Dr. Brajesh Kumar Gupta

Dr. Brajesh Kumar Gupta, known by the pen name "Mewadev," is a distinguished luminary in the literary world. He is the winner of Italian award '11th edition of the International Award of Excellence "Città del Galateo-Antonio De Ferrariis" 2024'. In 2023, he received the esteemed "APOLLON SIRMIENSIS" International Award in Serbia, alongside a special postage stamp issued by the state of Birland in his honour. His remarkable achievements include the prestigious Presidency of the International Prize De Finibus Terrae, dedicated to the memory of Maria Monteduro in Italy, and honorary doctorates in Literature from notable institutions in Serbia and Brazil.

I Want My Poetry to . . .
Through Every Culture

I want my poetry to the whole world
At the core of language, where civilizations intersect,
A span of lines, a gentle melody
Across each stanza, each line,
I and we create the harmony for all
We develop bonds, souls interlace
From far-off realms, with strong voices,
Our narratives are exchanged, and our realities reveal
In verses crafted from affection and elegance,
We perceive the world as a more secure environment
A composition of ideas, so extensive,
Where borders blur, and barriers are gone
In every chorus, a connection is formed,
A bridge of harmony, crafted without a weapon
With verses and beats, we rise high,
A unity that responds to the summons
For in our verse, we uncover the secret,
To unlock hearts and liberate minds
Thus, allow the lines to soar and gleam,
As we construct the connections, line by line
Across every culture, we will observe,
The strength of words to liberate us.

I want my poetry to . . . Volume 4
Tajalla Qureshi

Tajalla Qureshi - a literary enchantress who intertwines embroideries of thoughts and passions with the delicacy as a foremost artist in the realm of utterances. She is a gifted wordsmith from Pakistan. Like a shooting star, her literary presence blazes across the sky, leaving an indelible mark on the hearts and minds of all who encounter her work.

I Want My Poetry to . . .
Be the melody of your heart

I want my poetry to ravish and lavish
along with every nook of your essence
Heightens yet, profound in all its depth
as when they grace your lips, your tongue
my verses murmur, my heaven-like dreams
being under the luxury of florence and innocence
you whisper the love that remains unread,

I want my poetry to cuddle and clutch
at its most profound depth of delicacy
mirror the lumps, till when I write your name
a glittery feather smooches the slashes
when your eyes wipe up my deadly fears
Yet, the diligence devotes your devotion all near
unscripted scripts, unheard grips, musely mirths,

I want my poetry to sense and swim
all resonant under the ocean of your thoughts
with the muse, mumbles, and March mere
when your heart hears the heap of indulgence
Intensive and obsessive about the ownership I do
mine in my imaginations, fine up my fascinations
Severe the melodies are my promises I do to you,

I want my poetry to wrap and reveal
my magnificence under my hands to you,
When right away, holds high, heal the hues
letting loud vocals that I live for the loveliness in you
and wonders often when the night fades off
my divinity dwells in all the due, where you often flew
and I sip your left wine to grow and grew.

I want my poetry to . . . Volume 4

Abeera Mirza

"Writing is the tool of emotional healing." Abeera Mirza, English literature gold medalist, teacher, and poet, is a daughter of the Mughal empire from Pakistan. She's contributed to 200+ anthologies, won numerous awards, and serves as a jury member for Maverick Writing Community, India.

Email: abeera.quotes@gmail.com
Instagram|Facebook: @abeera_quotes

I Want My Poetry to . . .
Poetry Voice

I want my poetry to be the voice of the soul,
I want my poetry to play a significant role.

I pack echoes of emotions of the mind,
My poetry has a silent whisper of heart to find.

I want my poetry to be the voice of every heart,
With every heartbeat, my poem takes art.

I composed the moonlit musings in rhymes,
Words that rhyme are a chime in time.

I want my poetry to . . . Volume 4

Sotirios A. Christopoulos

Sotirios Christopoulos, son of Athanasios, was born in Thessaloniki. He has studied Theology, Pedagogy, Economics, and taught the latter. Sotirios is a writer of songs, poems, and stories. He created and leads the free expression and creation show *"What I Love"*: https://otiagapao.weebly.com/

I Want My Poetry to . . .
Teach Me a thing

I want my poetry to teach me a thing—
A spark that whispers in the hush of night,
A wild, untamed voice, still innocent,
That speaks in colors we've forgotten, bright.

I want my poetry to dig for treasure,
Where the soil's still soft, the roots unturned,
To find the joy that once ran like rivers,
The laughter of a child who never learned
To silence wonder, to lock it away,
To see the world through a lens of gray.

I want my poetry to be a secret,
A dance in the rain, a shadow on the wall,
The reckless joy of an untied shoelace,
A heart that beats without the fear of fall.

Teach me to see the world as new,
With crayons and dreams, not debts or dues,
To walk barefoot on a road unmarked,
With stars as guides and the moon as sparks.

I want my poetry to wake the child
Who ran through fields with dirt-streaked hands,
Who never counted time or felt it wild,
But let it slip like grains of golden sands.

I want my poetry to teach me light—
To be unbroken, unbound, unafraid,
To find the beauty in the simplest flight,
To be the child who dreams and never fades.

I want my poetry to . . . Volume 4
Errol D. Bean

Errol D. Bean / "The Thinking Bean" – is a Jamaican author, poet, singer/songwriter. Retired, Bean has consolidated over 40 years of creative writing for a forthcoming publication – *Elevated Livity: Poetic Reasoning and Nuggets of Wisdom.* Several of his poems have been by published by *Inner Child Press International*.

I Want My Poetry to . . .

    I want my poetry to…
be a catalyst to foster the spread and growth
of love, globally and universally
    (for you and me) –
love that motivates us to care, share and serve, sacrificially;
love manifested as tolerance, gentleness, and kindness;
love that stifles selfishness, envy and hatred

    I want my poetry to…
explore the tenets of sincere friendship
    (for you and me) –
tenets that *define the Privileges of Friendship,*
tenets that *explain the Parameters of Friendship,*
tenets that *extol the Power of Friendship,*
and tenets that *test the Pulse of Friendship*

    I want my poetry to…
flatten mountains, imagined or real;
tear down barriers, imagined or real;
    (for you and me) –
mountains that blur visions of world peace
barriers that block racial harmony

    I want my poetry to…
demolish delusions and illusions
    (for you and me) –
delusions and illusions that lead to psychosis,
delusions and illusions that set us up for
generational failures

    I want my poetry to…
conquer fear, imagined and real
    (for you and me) –
fear that:
dries our throats and makes us mumble like a goat;
bulges our eyes and makes our brilliant thought die;
tightens our chest and prevents us from doing our best!;
enfeebles our feet and makes us from simple tasks retreat!;
cripples our minds and makes the less gifted leave us behind

I want my poetry to . . . Volume 4

I want my poetry to…
inspire mindful acceptance of and conscious
adjustment to the natural stages of life – impact of longevity
    (for you and me) –
mindful acceptance and conscious adjustment when longevity
carves permanent timelines on our faces;
casts wrinkles on our skin;
scrapes crow's feet on eye corners from smiles;
reduces and *weakens* our bones,
attacks our self-confidence and
restructures physical beauty – contours and
curves, and causes *six pack* to get flat and flap.

    I want my poetry to…
straighten the jagged paths of the journey,
confront the treacherous "human bruit beasts" we encounter
    (for you and me) –
jagged paths that trip us up and cause us to lose our footing;
jagged paths that test our courage and cast doubt on our mission
treacherous "human bruit beasts" that cause us to stumble and
tarnish our integrity and reputation

    I want my poetry to…
expel negative energies and inspire positive livity –
(elevated spirituality)
    (for you and me) –
expel negative energies manifested in biases, prejudices,
and misogyny;
inspire positive livity that empowers us to always be in
Divine Energy

IF, ultimately, my *poetic reasoning* and creative musings
can inspire these outcomes, and more
    (for you and me) –
then, my poetic outflows and creative musings would
not be quickly erased
nor blown away by the powerful winds of time
during or after my time …

I want my poetry to . . . Volume 4
Hannie Rouweler

Hannie Rouweler (Netherlands, Goor, 13 June 1951), poet and translator, has been living in Leusden, the Netherlands since the end of 2012. Before she lived in different places in Holland, she also stayed abroad for a longer period of time. Her sources of inspiration are nature, love, loss, childhood memories and travel. In 1988 she made her debut with Regendruppels op het water (Raindrops on water). Since then, more than 40 collections of poetry have been published, also ten translations into various foreign languages.

I Want My Poetry to . . . published

I want my poems to be published so they don't rest
fading away in drawers, mice eat them, mold-affected paper,
because of overturned glasses of water and fruit juice
that regularly stand on my desk. I also eat there, on that spot,
with crumbs of bread left behind. At the computer and printer closeby.

Poems are to be read by everyone and tastes differ, to every person
something suits best, for anyone too like a cup fits with a saucer,
poems coincide with those who read them at strange and weird times
depending on what they like, at special events, and words exist
for those who don't find them so easily 1, 2, 3. Eye contact, eureka.

I want my poems to be published. In a proper book.
They can be read at breakfast, lunch, dinner
or in peace and quiet by a lampshade on the couch. Anywhere.
Poems are like birds, destination unknown, they know
no boundaries. They build nests together in trees, under roof tiles.

I want my poetry to... Volume 4

Tamikio L. Dooley

Author Tamikio L. Dooley is a multi award-winning author. She is the author of 150 titles and 100 published books. The author writes fiction and nonfiction of crime, thriller, mystery, fantasy, historical, western, romance, zombie apocalypse, and paranormal. In her spare time, she writes short stories, poetry, articles, essays, health books, and children's books, diaries, journals, inspiring books, culture, African American, and history books.

I Want My Poetry to…

'I Want My Poetry To,' accomplish inspiration,
Wisdom and knowledge,
For anyone willing to learn and listen,
Embrace the beauty of poetry.
A poet's artistic words,
'I Want My Poetry To,' instill love,
For those who struggle with poetry, there is still hope.
To put it artistically,
Injecting some vibrancy and flair,
I incorporate the essence of what I desire my poetry to convey.
Which is love, compassion, and warmth,
"I Want My Poetry To' unleash the craving of artistic words.

'I Want My Poetry To'… by Tamikio L. Dooley
'I Want My Poetry To,' accomplish inspiration,
Wisdom and knowledge,
For anyone willing to learn and listen,
Embrace the beauty of poetry.
A poet's artistic words,
'I Want My Poetry To,' instill love,
For those who struggle with poetry, there is still hope.
To put it artistically,
Injecting some vibrancy and flair,
I incorporate the essence of what I desire my poetry to convey.
Which is love, compassion, and warmth,
"I Want My Poetry To' unleash the craving of artistic words.

I want my poetry to . . . Volume 4

Ivan Pozzoni

Ivan Pozzoni was born in Monza in 1976. Between 2007 and 2024, 13 his poetry's books were published. He wrote 150 volumes, 1000 essays, founded an avant-garde movement (NéoN-avant-gardisme). His verses are translated into 25 languages. In 2024, he return to the artistic world and melts the *NSEAE Kolektivne* (New socio/ethno/aesthetic anthropology).

I Want My Poetry to . . .
tell about mathematics and geometry

I want my poetry
to tell about mathematics and geometry.
The ballad of Peggy and Pedro barked out by the punkbestials
of the Garibaldi Bridge, with a mixture of hatred and despair,
teaches us the intimate relationship between geometry and love,
to love as if we were maths surrounded by stray dogs.

Peggy you were drunk, normal mood,
in the slums along the bed of the Tiber
and alcohol, on August evenings, doesn't warm you up,
clouding every sense in annihilating dreams,
transforming every chewed-up sentence into a gunfight in the back
on armour dissolved by the summer heat.
Lying on the edges of the bridge's ledges,
among the drop-outs of the *Rome open city*,
you opened your heart to the gratuitous insult of Pedro,
your lover, and toppled over, falling into the void,
drawing gravitational trajectories from the sky to the cement.

Pedro wasn't drunk, a day's journey away,
you weren't drunk, abnormal state of mind,
in the slums along the bed of the Tiber,
or in the empty parties of Milan's movida,
with the intention of explaining to dogs and tramps
a curious lesson of non-Euclidean geometry.
Mounted on the edge of the bridge,
in the apathetic indifference of your distracted pupils,
you jumped, in the same trajectory of love,
along the same fatal path as your Peggy,
landing on the cement at the same instant.

The punkbestials of the Garibaldi Bridge, cleared by the local authority,
will spread a surreal lesson to every slum in the world
centred on the astonishing idea
that love is a matter of non-Euclidean geometry.

I want my poetry to . . . Volume 4
Huniie Parker

Huniie is a poet, spoken word artist, and life coach dedicated to inspiring growth and healing. Author of *No Longer a Slave* and *Diary of a Lonely Woman: My Cave*, she's toured with Max Parthas and Tribal Raine. Huniie also hosts *Poetic Xpressionz*, sharing stories that empower and uplift.

I Want My Poetry to…

I want my poetry…
 to wrap you in a cocoon Of feelings
I want my poetry to…
 make you think On a level you never have before
I want my poetry…
To take you out of your comfort zone
I want my poetry…
To bring you to your toes
I want my poetry to…
Slam you to the grown
I want my poetry to…
stir your emotions so to the point
You feel angry, mad, sad, happy, and joyful
I want my poetry to…
 make you ask how, can I correct this?
I want my poetry to…
make you feel alive
So alive that you make a difference
I want my poetry to…
Make a difference in your life
I want every letter, every syllable, and every word
To caress your mind & heart at the same time,
If my poetry can do this,
Then I Poet have done my job.

I want my poetry to... Volume 4

Marcelo Sánchez

Marcelo Sánchez writes poems, stories and essays. He was born in Buenos Aires, Argentina, and lives in Germany. His works have been selected for various magazines and literary anthologies.

I Want My Poetry to . . .

I want my poetry to
fill the blank page,
without me being afraid
of the blank page,
with me setting myself to write
only when I have an idea
of what to do.

The page that starts blank
is not yet a sheet of paper
nor a laptop screen,
it is inside me as are
the things I imagine and
about which I'll write.

I want my poetry to... Volume 4
Shoshana Vegh

Shoshana Vegh, an Israeli poet, a writer, an editor, a translator from English to Hebrew, a publisher. She wrote 24 books and edited over 200 as an editor. She established a house of publishing at 2009 by the name Pyutit.com.

I Want My Poetry to . . .

I want my poetry to be as a medicine
A few drops of compassion
Green leaves of hope
Sunny moments to cure the wounds
I want my lyrics metaphorically
replace my visits to the medical center
The ill and the sadness can stay at the poetry but after
I want the flowers to grow and to be wild
At my when the poem is ready
I want it to be possible to move all the dark and to bright the days
It is said that words can make another world a better one
with great happiness I want my poetry to take me there

I want my poetry open the hearts for more love

I want my poetry to . . . Volume 4

Akleema Ali

Akleema Ali is a Reiki Master Teacher from Trinidad & Tobago. Her passion is on using Reiki as a major modality for optimal health & wellness. Her mission is encouraging others to build their own sanctuary. Her vision is everyone can access peace within.

I Want My Poetry to . . .

I want my poetry to express the words I could not say in the real world.
I want my poetry to add colour to the landscape of those in hope of love, peace, creativity and soulful moments.
I want my poetry to bleed into humanity seeking positive change with every syllable.

I want my poetry to become the hope for peace and kindness for the New Earth.
I want my poetry to have the rhythm of oneness where no discrimination and injustice exists.
I want my poetry to speak volumes and inspire others to do good.

I want my poetry to free people from their mental distress and loneliness.
I want my poetry to teach others that communication and expression is important.
I want my poetry to express that there are no boundaries in writing and feeling.

I want my poetry to become the legacy that is left for the younger generation.
I want my poetry to represent an individual's full potential and to never give up.
I want my poetry to be the plaster for people's soul wrenching wounds.

I want my poetry to close all barriers and obstacles for people from different lands.
I want my poetry to be the forever bridge for calmness and serenity.
I want my poetry to bring peace and love to all of humanity.

I want my poetry to . . . Volume 4

Hussein Habasch

Hussein Habasch is a poet from Afrin, Kurdistan. He currently lives in Bonn, Germany. Born in 1970 in Şiyê town. His poems have been translated into more than 35 languages, and has had his poetry published in a large number of international poetry anthologies, more than 150 anthologies. He has a large number of books, many of which have been translated into international languages such as English, Spanish, French, Chinese, Romanian... He participated in many international festivals of poetry […]

I Want My Poetry to . . .

I want my poetry to be coats, sweaters and blankets for children in refugee camps in this harsh winter.
I want my poetry to be a violin that blows the sweetest melodies for lovers and passers-by.
I want my poetry to be an open road, if only once, that leads me to my mother to kiss her hands and put my tired head on her chest before I die!
I want my poetry to be a handkerchief that wipes the sweat from my father's forehead as he returns from work.
I want my poetry to be a rose on my beloved's chest or a unique perfume that always smells from her long neck.
I want my poetry to be a cloud of rain that falls on a thirsty land.
I want my poetry to be a dove of peace that flutters over the whole world.
I want my poetry to be a light at the end of the tunnel...
I want my poetry to be a sun and a mountain exchanging love, laughter, poems and madness.
I want my poetry to be an olive field like the olive fields in Afrin!
I want my poetry to be a tree, where two lovebirds exchange love on its branches.
I want my poetry to be a medicine box for a sick person
A loaf of bread for a hungry person
A crutch for an old man
And a chair for a crippled person.
I want my poetry to be eyes for the blind
A tongue for a mute
And ears for the deaf.
I want my poetry to be five euros
In the pocket of a homeless person!

I want my poetry to... Volume 4

Lilla Latus

Lilla Latus (Poland) - poetess, translator, author of reviews, song lyrics, articles about travelling and social issues. Many times awarded both for her poetry and engagement in cultural activity for local community. Published nine books of poems. Her poetry has been published in many magazines and anthologies, both in Poland and abroad.

I Want My Poetry to . . .

to dwell in the heart of mystery -
a fragile, timeless breath,
a seed of immortality

to speak with the voice of unseen things -
fleeting light and whispering winds
slipping through the cracks of solitude

to fight like a stray dog -
hungry, wounded,
but too stubborn to die

I want my poetry to... Volume 4
Gordana Sarić

Gordana Sarić, from Montenegro, professor of French, author of 25 books of love and children's poetry and prose. Her 30 poems about letters are taught in Primary School. She is the winner of many world awards and is an ambassador of culture and peace in many countries.

Awards, Giant of World Culture from Mexico, Divine Woman for Excellence in Italy, Awards for Culture in Morocco, Peru, Spain, etc.

I Want My Poetry to . . .

I would like my poetry to be a prayer for peace and love
dashing and elegant full of inner glow
to radiate the breath of an angel with an aura of purity
and the warmth of it unites yearning hearts.

I want it to be magical soul music
a beacon of timeless love,
source of tenderness and blissful blinks,
creator of a world where goodness is celebrated.

To be enchanted with the breath of heaven
full of spring, dreams and light,
to be woven from eternal longings and desires
shining on the luminous throne of tenderness.

I would like the poem whose breath I breathe
leave my name among the stars
to exist as a blessing from God
and forever shines with the flame of love.

Translated By Diana Repas

I want my poetry to . . . Volume 4
Swayam Prashant

Swayam Prashant (pen name of Dr. Prashanta Kumar Sahoo) was born in the undivided Cuttack District, Odisha. He was formerly an Associate Professor of English, Sarupathar College, Assam, India. He has written ten books including *Joy of Love*; *Heart of Love* (poetry) (published in USA) and *The Sky Conquerors*.
www.facebook.com/swayamprashant.prashant
Email ID : swayam.prashant2001@gmail.com

I Want My Poetry to . . .

I Want My Poetry to Be . . .
the Embodiment of Truth, Goodness and Beauty
I want my poetry to bring
joy and peace to every soul –
to quell the restless,
to warm up the cold,
to give hope to the hopeless
and energize the old.
I want my poetry to show
the path in the pathless woods,
the solution to the labyrinth of life,
the hidden beauty in every object
and the sleeping lion in every soul.
And above all
I want my poetry to be
the medium through which
'nada brahmah'* (the sound divine) and 'sabda brahmah'* (the word divine)
manifest themselves
and my poetry, in all totality, becomes
the embodiment
of satyam* (Truth), shivam* (Goodness) and sundaram* (Beauty).

N.B. *Those marked with stars are Sanskrit words from Indian philosophy.*

I want my poetry to... Volume 4
Poul Lynggaard Damgaard

Poul Lynggaard Damgaard, born 24th of December, 1977, grew up in Odder, and lives in Aarhus, Denmark. His work appears in publications and anthologies world wide. He has participated in several International Poetry Festivals in the world, and his poetry has been translated to many different languages. He has been awarded a prize "Lyre of Orpheus" at the International Festival of Poetry-Orpheus, 2018. The International best poet of the year 2021. International poetry and Translation Centre, China.

I Want My Poetry to . . . sense

I want my poetry to sense.
Sensing is not aesthetics, but understanding. I am only welcome if I know that I am on behalf of others.
Sensing is not the aesthetic, because then reality is already written down. Aesthetics is sensing.
They were given the anchor, but those who were given both the ship and the anchor wanted it to be poetry, and reality was already gone. Everything is without reason, and everyone is without reason.
The creaking addition of the historical consciousness of the equation.
The object's creation of legal history. That two appeared as the same in the same. The creation of words by legal history.
If one's religious beliefs are not dependent on democracy, then there is nowhere to go. 8 days. Placebo changes horses, and the one who falls off the horse is himself a runestone.
The ones stopping one by one.
Leap years are strengthened immune defenses.
24 families and 184 family members.
A star above the crescent moon that moves apart in the night sky.
Earth is pure sand.
There is no danger of revealing the state secret as long as the tulip is a secret.
The dolmen's custody hidden in an opening. Hidden opening. Forgotten opening.
Forgotten breathing. Hannah Arendt.

I want my poetry to . . . Volume 4
Smruti Ranjan Mohanty

Smruti Ranjan Mohanty is a widely read and renowned Indian English poet, essayist, and writer from Odisha, known for his reflective and philosophical poetry. His works often delve into themes of life, spirituality, human emotions, and the complexities of existence. He has written extensively on topics such as self-awareness, simplicity, and the transient nature of life. Many of his poems, like those from his series A Look at Life, Something I Look at, The Journey, The Rivulet etc. emphasize introspection and finding meaning in everyday experiences. His write ups are well accepted and widely read across the world.

I Want My Poetry to . . .

I want my poetry to live with my dream and reality
Poetry is a beautiful dream
On a sleepless summer night
That comes with a smile.
When you are silently dozing
Poetry is the hope in the eyes
Of someone terminally ill.
Poetry is a ray of light
Amidst darkness, frustration, and apathy.

Poetry is life
That puts death at bay.
Poetry is the eternal spring that drives
The hot summer away.
Poetry is the beauty of childhood
The spirit of youth and the stay of old age

Poetry is that unusual summer shower
That drenches your body and mind
When you feel exhausted and out of the world.
Poetry is mother's lap
And father's shadow
Sister's Rakhi on your hand
Friend's heart, brother's love and concern
The voice of Bulbul in a dry desert.

Poetry is a lovely pair of eyes
That waits for you for hours
The quivering lips
Locked with yours
And the waves of dimples writing
The lyric of love and romance

Poetry is grace and beauty undefined
The eyes of the blind and
The voice of the dumb
The love of the old man for his wife
Their undefined chemistry

I want my poetry to... Volume 4

The passion and feeling that saw them
Through the years of their life.

Poetry is a beautiful garden
The beauty of which never fades
The perennial stream
That never dries up
The symphony of love
That always murmurs
The innate urge that sustains existence
Pushes life to fight for its own survival.

Poetry is the story of mankind
Its ebb and tide, fighting against circumstances
To come to the zenith.
Poetry is life.
Its beauty, contradictions, and intricacies.
Poetry is the will, force, and
Means for survival against all odds.
When there is darkness everywhere
Poetry, as a ray of hope, shines in my eyes.
Holds me, beats in the heart of heart.

As an ocean of hope, it tells me emphatically
Go ahead; the victory is yours.
That which sustains existence
Uplifts and fulfils life
Takes you to new horizons
To different levels of consciousness
That which is always with you
Irrespective of your situation
And state of mind is poetry.

That which brings you close to life
Faithfully reflects you, your surroundings
Your joy and anguish are poetry.
Poetry is not all about love and romance
Nature and its beauty, rhythm, and rhyme
Poetry is living with the reality.
Accepting life as it is

I want my poetry to . . . Volume 4

Ifeanyi Enoch Onuoha

Ifeanyi Enoch Onuoha is a ghostwriter, author, pastor, and facilitator of positive change. His works are known for improving lives. He resides in Owerri, Imo State, Nigeria, with his beautiful wife and daughter.

I Want My Poetry to . . .

I want my poetry to be a life-transforming tool. An inspiration that encourages humanity to meet each other's needs and eliminate greed.
I want my poetry to give you the audacity, intensity, tenacity, integrity, and vitality to bring your dreams to life.
I want my poetry to inspire writers to create meaningful work that motivates, challenges, and educates readers.
I want my poetry to provide insights that encourage you to unleash the greatness within you.
I want my poetry to act as a catalyst for your rebirth, inspiring you to strive for personal growth and improvement.
I want my poetry to be the truth that prompts your conscience to uphold justice and reject vices that destroy lives.
I want my poetry to serve as a bridge connecting the ancient with the modern, allowing people of all ages to sharpen their creative edges and enrich their lives.
I want my poetry to be the light that enlightens minds and brightens places.
I want my poetry to be a healing balm for broken hearts and wounded souls.
I want my poetry to announce the good news that awakens you to a glorious day full of possibilities.
I want my poetry to provide the enlightenment that helps people escape the prison of poverty and enter the palace of prosperity.
I want my poetry to break the limiting beliefs that have bound individuals and open the door to a world of possibilities.
I want my poetry to be the voice of change that quiets the noise of challenges faced by individuals and communities.
I want my poetry to be the hope for those in desperate situations.
I want my poetry to blaze a trail for a better life for everyone.
I want my poetry to be the vehicle that takes you to a land of peace, progress, and abundance.
I want my poetry to be known and remembered for the transformative change it brings to listeners and readers.
I want my poetry to be the lifebuoy that saves people from drowning in the challenges of life.
I want my poetry to be the oil that lubricates your creative wheels and propels you toward success.
I want my poetry to provide you with the knowledge and strength you need to excel in life's race.
I want my poetry to grant you peace of mind, ensuring good health and long life.

I want my poetry to . . . Volume 4

Marlon Salem Gruezo

Marlon Salem Gruezo is a Filipino-Spanish peace and culture advocate, and arts & letters protagonist, and a member of some notable international non-government organisations whose core missions are peace, culture , arts and education promotions. A poetry enthusiast, writer and editor of several international online and print magazines.

I Want My Poetry to…

I want my poetry to dance in the moonlight,
To whisper secrets in the hush of night,
To paint the sky with hues of dawn,
And cradle hearts that feel forlorn.

I want my poetry to sing with the breeze,
To rustle leaves on ancient trees,
To echo in the chambers of the soul,
And make the broken feel whole.

I want my poetry to blaze like fire,
To kindle dreams and spark desire,
To weave a tapestry of light,
And guide the lost through darkest night.

I want my poetry to flow like streams,
To carry whispers of forgotten dreams,
To carve its path through stone and sand,
And leave its mark on every land.

I want my poetry to soar on wings,
To touch the stars and all their rings,
To dive into the ocean's deep,
And in its depths, my secrets keep.

I want my poetry to heal and mend,
To be a faithful, lifelong friend,
To speak the words we dare not say,
And light the path to a brighter day.

I want my poetry to bloom and grow,
To be the warmth in winter's snow,
To be the voice of silent cries,
And wipe the tears from weary eyes.

I want my poetry to live and breathe,
To be the air that hearts can seethe,
To be the love that never fades,
And shine through life's most shadowed glades.

I want my poetry to... Volume 4

Dr. Biswas

Dr. Biswas (78), a Bengali poet, nature loving person. During his teenage, edited a literary publication *'BANASABHA'* (meeting within forest) with self effort. Achieved National and international literally award. Associated in different literary groups. Participated as a speaker in National and International seminars at home and abroad.

I Want My Poetry to . . .

I want my poetry to stand by the roadside
For shelter within the tent of a poverty stricken
I want my poetry to serve for the beauty of nature
I want my poetry to help the child who like to be blossomed
I want my poetry to move around the world
For peace and sovereignty which is missing day by day
I want my poetry to stay with the poets not with the politicians
I want my poetry to search solitary river
By the side of which miles after miles I can walk.

I want my poetry to... Volume 4

Marion de Vos-Hoekstra

Marion de Vos-Hoekstra was born in the Netherlands and is married to a career diplomat. They both served in North Yemen, Tanzania, United Kingdom, Mali, Spain, South Africa and The United States and now in the Netherlands. She trained as a teacher of French and as translator French, English and Dutch. She is also fluent in Spanish and German, plays the piano and the guitar, is amateur ornithologist and makes drawings, aquarelles and oil paintings. Nature, human nature and her nomad life are her main inspirations. She attended several poetry workshops in English among which a Masterclass in New York at Poetshouse and a workshop at the prestigious 92Y Institute. She is the author of five poetry collections (in English and Dutch), 4 with Demer Press, and is published in several anthologies and magazines (25) all over the world. (South Africa, Australia, UK and US).

I Want My Poetry to . . .

I want my poetry to
flow like a stream of lava
solidify in the memory
of my readers

I want my poetry to
be a treasure hunt
a road map to the
diamond in core

I want my poetry to
galop at the rhythm
of a galloping horse
manes flying free

I want my poetry to
fly like a migrating bird
from North to South
from East to West

I want my poetry to
be a home, a shelter
for wisdom
comfort and consolation.

I want my poetry to . . . Volume 4

Ibrahim Honjo

Ibrahim Honjo is a poet/writer. He has published 41 books. His poems have been published in over 80 worldwide anthologies, and over 60 literary newspapers, magazines, radio, and TV stations. Some of his poems have been translated and published into 21 languages. He received numerous awards for his written word and creativity.

I Want My Poetry to . . .
Message of poetry

I want my poetry to…
speak loudly
that its speech can be heard far away
and wake up those who decide
about the fate of mankind

I write about lives
I wish to remind myself and all people
how we live our lives
how we abuse lives
with different tensions
which have the function to destroy people's life
in the name of creator of all worlds

collage images of my poetry
are often pictures of real life
life burden that I care about
as many other people

every day, I ask myself
about emotional and mental relationship
with the heated reality
which left trace in distant past
but without the answer to all questions

my poetry is a summary of my journey
my experience and many other people
and a reminder of how we live in this world
to a world that is sometimes almost dialectical
and extremely beautiful
sometimes just rubble

question is
how to find a shock absorber
that can withstand the blows
of the rushing future
and human madness

I want my poetry to . . . Volume 4

life is a mixture of optimism
pessimism
criticism of existing misconceptions
and illusions of modern humanity

I would like my poetry to awaken love
in every human being

I want wars to end forever
and that these verses reach all war makers
because only they can make and maintain peace

poetry is only a reminder

I want my poetry to stay that way

I want my poetry to . . . Volume 4
Tyran Prizren Spahiu

Tyran Prizren Spahiu was born Kosovo and he graduated with a degree in English Language and Literature at Prishtina University-Kosovo. He was awarded Poet of the year by Pegasus Albania. He authored six novels, and twenty three Poetic Verses books in addition to Dream Language English Grammar-Visual English Dictionary. He is a wonderful, passionate, artist, he possesses deep knowledge and high literary skills in the art of prose.

I Want My Poetry to . . .
Bloodiness In The World!

To write about love, lust of ecstasy. morning light
dance of the stars
outdoor beauty
virgin source
peacocks, roses
NO
I can not!
Dried are my tears
feelings are amputated!
*
Continuing downhill, I do fell smell of cadavers
this moment, tomorrow
I know, it will move on
my soul is suffering
to run away
bloodiness in the world
fed with hate
they, medieval minds prisoners
pouring out animal lust
killing, violating, blood shedding
raping creatures of the Great Creator
at this very moment
on the dawn of the sad day
the sun radiates memories
children are massacred
closed are eyes
POET is ashamed
disgraced is the world of the human race!
*
Great Lord. In this mess, PLEASE
SAVE THE BEST RACE, the PEOPLE!

I want my poetry to... Volume 4
Ngozi Olivia Osuoha

Ngozi Olivia Osuoha is a Nigerian poet, writer, thinker, hymnist, and an award winning anthologist. She has authored 28 poetry books, all published outside Nigeria. She has published over 350 poems, articles and essays in over 50 countries. Some of her pieces have been translated in over 16 languages. She has some books in foreign libraries including the US Library of Congress. She is Best Of The Net and Pushcart Nominees. She is a graduate of Estate Management, with some experience in Banking, Broadcasting and tailoring.

I Want My Poetry to . . .

I want my poetry to heal the world.
Sick people need succour and homeless folks need shelter,
I want my poetry to be both succour and shelter to them.
There is hunger and famine,
I want my poetry to be food both to the poor and rich.
The world is devastated and ruined,
I want my poetry to give hope and future to all.
War is ravaging the earth,
Racism, extremism and terrorism are pulling down humanity,
I want my poetry to unite mankind and give creatures beautiful faces once again.
I want my poetry to immortalize faith, peace, love, kindness and development.
I want my poetry to be a holy book, let it preach God's universal sovereignty and mastery.

I want my poetry to... Volume 4
Aleksandra Sołtysiak

Aleksandra Sołtysiak (Poland) graduate of the Catholic University of Lublin and Jagiellonian University in Kraków. She has served as coeditor of the poetry anthology Dotyk nadziei („The Touch of Hope"), which was translated into Ukrainian and German, as well as of the international anthology in support of world peace „ The tree of peace turns green/European poetry for universal harmony", which has been translated into Polish and English. She is also the author „Hope blossoms longer" and the published poetry volume „Spilled from the cases". […]

I Want My Poetry to . . .

I want my poetry to
taste like brambles.
To bring out joy in yours
look, and the thorns of pain
enchased it in brass.

To resemble ours
endless conversations.
I drew from them inspiration
to the next verses,
name – you put it between them.

They cling to you and
I embrace your shoulders. In a magic
mosaic of words, the day has frozen,
until you gave birth to love in me –
it lasts forever.

I earnestly gather thier crumbs
in the hospital room when – together
with hidden bramble juice –
I drank your sapphire name.

The angel has extinguished the candle flame…

Translated by Olga Smolnytska (Ukraine)

I want my poetry to . . . Volume 4
Rahim Karim (Karimov)

Rahim Karim (Karimov) - Uzbek-Russian-Kyrgyz poet, writer, publicist, translator (b. 1960, Osh, Kyrgyzstan). Graduated from the Moscow Literary Institute named after A.M. Gorky (1986). Member of the National Union of Writers, the Union of Journalists of the Kyrgyz Republic. Nominee for the Nobel Prize in Literature and Peace for 2023, 2024.

I Want My Poetry to . . .

I want my poetry to become swallows,
And make a nest in every heart in the springtime.
I want my poems to become doves,
And spread peace throughout the Earth.

I want my poems to become cranes,
And embrace all of Humanity with a flock of happiness.
I want my poems to become nightingales,
And embrace the entire globe with songs of love.

I want my poems to become clouds,
And illuminate the entire blue sky.
I want my poems to become birds of Happiness,
And be in the hands of every person on the Planet.

I want my poetry to . . . Volume 4

Tống Thu Ngân

Tống Thu Ngân is a poetess. She was born in Vietnam. She grew up in Ho Chi Minh city, Vietnam. She is a lecturer of The Ho Chi Minh City University of Padagogy. Her pen name is Mimosa Tím. She has dual Vietnamese and American citizenship. She started writing poetry in 2014, and to date she has written 1,916 poems. She is a social activist. Most of her poems are written in a free style, allegorical style, with diverse themes of love for the homeland, romantic love, humanity, building social ethics, inspiring people, giving good messages for life, solidarity between peoples, enhancing the cultural identity of her country and contributing to integrating her national culture with the developed culture of the world. In particular, her poems praise peace and oppose war, contributing to building a peaceful world, love for humanity, social ethics, for a good life, and common prosperity.[…]

I Want My Poetry to . . . be

I want my poetry to be a raindrop
To wash away all the dust of the world
My poetry to be pure tears, washing away all sorrows,
Bringing faith, love, hope, for a new life for everyone

I want my poetry to be a ray of morning sunshine,
To illuminate life, dispelling all the clouds.
To warm the heart, and illuminate the path,
To bring everyone to the shore of happiness

I want my poetry to be the murmuring sound of waves,
Bringing joy, laughter, and hope.
The call of the sea, reminding us to live,
Bringing strength, overcoming all challenges.

I want my poetry to be a gentle lullaby,
Bringing good sleep, and beautiful dreams.
 Mother's loving words, warm and gentle,
Bringing a sense of security, without worry to her children

I want my poems to be blooming flowers,
Bringing a fragrant scent, making life more beautiful.

The flower of love, blooming in everyone's heart
Bringing happiness, and endless joy.

I want my poems to beautify life
Contributing to repelling war, bringing peace everywhere,
Bringing love to all mankind
Oh how beautiful are these wonderful poems...

I want my poetry to... Volume 4
Izabela Zubko

Izabela Zubko is a Polish poetess, journalist and translator; an author of 16 volumes of poetry. She is a member of the Polish Writers' Union, the Polish Authors' Association and the Association of Culture Originators in Warsaw. Her poems were published in many newspapers in Poland and abroad.

I Want My Poetry to . . .

... permeate the parched earth like rain
become a whisper of leaves in the wind
and twinkling light on the water mirror

... dwell in human hearts
be an invisible pier
leading to the peaceful shore

where beauty marks out simple paths

Translated by Anna Maria Stępień

I want my poetry to . . . Volume 4

Mark Andrew Heathcote

Mark Andrew Heathcote is an adult learning difficulties support worker. His poems have been published in journals, magazines, and anthologies online and in print. He is from Manchester and resides in the UK. Mark is the author of "In Perpetuity" and "Back on Earth," two books of poems published by Creative Talents Unleashed.

I Want My Poetry to . . .
Whatever I write . . .

Whatever I write, whatever my themes
I want my poetry to speak of a man of dreams.
Not of a man of political regimes
While everyone around me either laughs or screams

I want my poetry to reject the nonsense of being the same.
There's no one I know who's to blame.
They're all as blind or deaf as my neighbor next door.
Whatever you like darling or love, it's all a dying repertoire.

It's all an after-show, an encore selfishly desired.
Or inconsiderately dying, just lying
Bleeding on the page—as if giving up life was required.
As if giving up loving, giving up caring was truly edifying.

As if giving up my words, as if giving up poetry
It would be more - hip and have a better handle.
And we'd all be better off dead with a bullet of lead.
Then read what some prophet said as our next protégé.

Darling, whatever you like, I'll write to you.
Gentle or proud, egotistical and loud
I'll write for you; I'll write for you.
Darling, you are a creation. creation

Darling, all you said is make me proud and glad.
I am tired of being bored.
Wondering what it's all been for.
Oh, I want you to write poetry everybody talks about.

And take it home, darling, darling, I want you to touch my soul.
And wheeled a blunt axe backstage.
And tell me it's always been you.
And you say, what's been me? ' And I say worship and poetry.

The loose threads on your dress
Everything you do and speak. I guess.

I want my poetry to... Volume 4

As if philanthropical worship past the dawn
Will answer all my calls, all my prayers predawn.

Whatever I write, whatever my themes
I want my poetry to speak of a man of dreams.
Not of a man of political regimes
Because when the sunsets or rises everything gleams.

I want my poetry to . . . Volume 4

Tanja Ajtic

Tanja Ajtic from Serbia and Canada. She is a poet, writer and a freelance artist. Her poems have been published in more than 200 collections, anthologies, and magazines in eleven languages. She has published a book of poetry "Contours of Love". She is the winner of many awards and diplomas.

I Want My Poetry to . . .

I want my poetry to
reach you.
To arrive at your sigh
and for the conclusion of the poem
to be your breath
my dear.
Writing to you is a pleasure
that unlocks the doors to happiness,
unfurling all the sunflowers in the field
and propelling them toward the Sun
of love.
To think of you is a delightful
mental dance of my
nerve endings,
which are always taut
and sensitive when I am with you,
my beloved.
In this contemporary world
where flames ascend to the heavens
and the sky collapses upon the earth,
I long for my
poetry to reach you,
for I do not wish to dwell
in despair.

I want my poetry to . . . Volume 4

Noreen Ann Snyder

Noreen Ann Snyder is a poet and a published author of five poetry books and four of them are co-authored with her loving husband, Garry A. Snyder. She is the founder of The Poetry Club on Facebook. garryandnoreensnyder.wixsite.com/poetry

I Want My Poetry to...

I want my poetry to
convey the truth and nothing but the truth
no matter what other people say.
I want my poetry to
make a difference, be powerful,
be enlightening, uplifting and encouraging.

I want my poetry to
make you smile and laugh,
to cry a bucketful of tears
to cause you to be angry and
be part of the solution.

I want my poetry to
give a voice to the voiceless,
to cause them to come out of their shells
screaming, "I have a voice too!
I want to be heard! We matter!

I want my poetry to
cause you to stand up for
what you believe in.
Not to be ashamed.

I want my poetry to
cause you to believe
in love, true love.
It's powerful! Just believe!

I want my poetry to
convince you not to give up.
Don't die! The world needs you,
we need you!
Hold on, tomorrow might be brighter.

I want my poetry to
convey you to live your dreams,

I want my poetry to . . . Volume 4

believe in your dreams.
Make it happen! Don't listen to others!

But most important of all, but not the least,
I want my poetry to convey you that God and Jesus
are real and alive. Believe, just believe.

I want my poetry to... Volume 4
Aziz Mountassir

Aziz Mountassir is a Moroccan poet and champion for peace and the uplifting of humanity. Mr. Mountassir is a very influential poet and ambassador who lends himself to the one and all.

I Want My Poetry to . . .

I want my poetry to be a gentle breeze,
A whisper of hope that puts hearts at ease.
With every word, I seek to impart,
The warmth of compassion, the beat of one heart.

In a world so vast, let love be the thread,
Weaving connections, where once there was dread.
Let my verses dance like petals in spring,
Celebrating the joy that true friendship can bring.

I want my poetry to paint skies so blue,
To blossom like flowers, in every hue.
Where peace is the anthem, and kindness the song,
A melody sweet, where we all can belong.

In rhythms of unity, let my lines flow,
Bridging the chasms, where understanding can grow.
For every soul searching for solace and light,
I want my poetry to guide them each night.

So let it be known, with each heartfelt plea,
That love is the answer, and peace is the key.
I want my poetry to echo through time,
Reminding us all that together, we climb.

With verses united, let's rise above strife,
Crafting a tapestry of love in our life.
I want my poetry to be a soft spark,
Igniting a fire, a light in the dark.

I want my poetry to . . . Volume 4
Irena Jovanović

Irena Jovanović, born in 1971. in Zaječar, Serbia, Europe. She is a Master of Ceramics Design, a painter, and a poet writing in Serbian and English. She has held 20 solo art exhibitions in her country and created and is a leader of a Poetesses club "Blade"(of grass) in her hometown with 30 members. "Inner Child Press" published her First Poetry Book „Let it Be" in 2013, and she is widely represented in many world anthologies and magazines with her poetry in English.

I Want My Poetry to . . .

I want my poetry to open the universal understanding
of universes of verses within everyone's mind and soul
resolute to transverse many obstacles in various ways
a whole new approach to enlightenment to offer widely
not depending on any previous wildly concluded facts
in fact, I want to speak mildly in soothing waves
bringing new dimensions of bliss and ecstatic joy
reaching exalted peak of true love and divine realm
I want my poetry to become a balm and let all shine
intertwined with ease and breeze and butterflies flight
delight of beauty and splendor and refined glide
sliding in light of miraculous ways to speak alined
to the most crucial essence a person can find here
in the world which does not listen, I pray it can merely
try to hear a message of tiny but adorable words that melt
in a heartfelt ocean of magical whispers of inner sprite
I want my words to have a visionary, heavenly insights
in times that come to help reunite the passengers through time
primarily keep the peace all around, melodies of bells
let my letters tell all the most blissful and divine spells
of uplifted time, when we are all fine, calm, and sublime

I want my poetry to . . . Volume 4
Naheed Akhtar

Naheed Akhtar is an Academic and a bilingual Poet, currently teaching it Bharat Institute of Engineering and Technology, Hyderabad, India. Her published works- "Phatasms of My Heart", "The Earth's Love", "The Morphine", "Beyond the Clouds" and "Let the Womb Hold and Other Poems". He next book is slated this year. Her poems have been published in several international and national magazines.

She has been speaking at various platforms that include "Kolkata National Book Fair" and "The Festival Letter, Sahitya Akademi, Delhi".

She can be reached at
naheedakhtar123119@gmail.com
9618460045

I Want My Poetry to...

I want my poetry to...
Sensitize sensibility that is sleeping,
Energize empathy that's near extinction;

It must extend meaningfulness
To the ideas garbed in chaotic mindset,
Prevailing dichotomy in human minds;

I want it to...
Speak to each one of us
For one is the class, creed and type;

It must invite individuals
For the celebration of women's wombs
Whether they hold a boy or even a girl;
It must smoothe the pathways
From prejudices for women and even men

I want my poetry to...
Inject humanity in humans;
Spreading God's desired deeds
That make the earth heaven
Much before they reaches the heaven above

I want my poetry to . . . Volume 4
Gail Weston Shazor

Gail Weston Shazor is fond of the arcane, unusual and the not yet words.

Gail is more than accomplished in everything from Shakespearean sonnets to newly created styles. Gail Weston Shazor has authored several books along with numerous anthology contributions. Look for her on Inner Child Press.

I Want My Poetry to . . .

I want my poetry to
Eat popsicles
In the middle of winter
On a screened in back porch
While wearing mittens
Swiping at a cold and runny nose

I want my poetry to
Find the books left in attics
From your grandmother
Written in old English
And signed in cursive
With real leather bindings

I want my poetry to
Collect leaves
In late autumn
Before the icicles find nests
Along the spines
That glimmer for the sun

I want my poetry to
Find that God sized
Space inside of you
So that you may
Always be in wonder
At the minutia of life

I want my poetry to... Volume 4
Gregoire Marshall

Gregoire Marshall is the founder of Invincible Truth. He is a son, Brother, Partner, Father, and a Survivor, who grew up gay, with all the trials and tribulations that go along with that life experience. Humbly Grateful for the Miracles and Manifestations, he spent the past four years in University to develop his online courses to find one's Invincible Truth, going back through the Inner Child's Journey. For more information check out his website for written stories, which lead by example to in depth of introspection needed to heal and forgive one and others in the trauma journey. http://www.invincibletruth,org@gmail.com

I Want My Poetry to . . .

I want my Poetry to be a reflection and testimony to the song of my Life
I remember the moment I was frightened
I remember the moment I felt safe
I remember the moment I felt grace
I remember moments of exuberance
I remember the moment I felt defeated. I want my poetry help have the strength to begin again.
I remember the moment claimed my worth
I remember losing the father that made me feel disgrace. I want my poetry help me remember this saving grace
I was my art help me remember the tenderness in my mothers tears when she had to say goodbye
I remember holding the child intended to take my place.
I remember the brother that denied my face.
I remember the urge to help those in my same place.
I remember when I thought the Universe gave me grace I want my poetry yo help me remember the insecurity changed me forever when I realized I was meant to be the grace.
I remember being takeaway
I remember when the thought of another day was not in my place. I want my poetry remind me the precious moment I had learned to take for granted
I want my poetry to remind me those moments are a saving Grace
I remember the moment the 100-balloon float to the sky on the year remembering the day my daughter grace my life.
I remember the moment my daughter mom and I said goodbye.
I want my poetry to put to lyric those days of beauty and Grace
I remember the strength that told me I could fly.
I remember moments shared with souls that lost their place.
I remember the moment that money couldn't take the place of moments that came anyway.
I remember moments of isolation
I want my poetry to give hope to those who lost their way.
I want my poetry to show the promise of better days
I remember the moment of warm loving hands.
I remember moments of confusion
I remember moments of confidence
I remember moments of desperation
I remember moments of strength that could move mountains.

I want my poetry to... Volume 4

I want my poetry to tell the obstacles the got in my way.
I want my poetry to inspire to overcoming all obstacles in time
I remember moments with tears when I lost someone close to me.
I remember moments of Angels by my side
I remember moments when I knew I would never give up
I want my poetry to sooth the moment when Love means letting go.
I must now thread these moments to find the answer why
I remember all these moments
I want my poetry to be a testimonial to inspire one's Soul to never gave up.

I want my poetry to... Volume 4
Nour elhouda Guerbaz

Nour elhouda Guerbaz has a Master degree in semiotics Doctor of Arabic Literature and is professor of Arabic Narratives Mohamed Keidar University Biskra – Algeria TEECHNICAL Committee of the Modern Literary Renaissance Cultural ambassador at Advisor Peoples Academy of National an Uruguay Associate member of modern Literature Latin

I Want My Poetry to . . .

I want my poetry to be an olive branch for peace,
a rose for love and harmony,
a sincere word said to cheer up a little child tired by the days
and to make happy a homeland exhausted by pain and illness.
I want my poetry to be a symbol of freedom, happiness,
Brotherhood and security.
I want my poetry to be a token of love for humanity everywhere.
I want my poetry to be a prayer of love to God because God is love.
I want my poetry to be a bouquet of patience sprinkled on the heart
of every person in pain and burdened by the pain of the days.
I want my poetry to be a bridge of communication for joy,
Brotherhood and security.
I want my poetry to be a story told over time
about an Arab poet who refuses to surrender,
reconciled with all spectrums and religions,
her motto being love and spreading the culture of tolerance.
I want my poetry to be a beacon
for peoples and a popular story told by thousands of narrators passing
between my papers fleeing in this vast horizon.
I want my poetry to be a homeland for words that unite all arts.

I want my poetry to . . . Volume 4
Mohamed Abdel Aziz Shameis

Mohamed Abdel Aziz Shameis is the Founder of literary Renaissance School of Literature and Secretary-General of the Literary School, Cultural Activity of the International Union for the Children of Egypt.

Cultural Ambassador at Inner Child Press International
Ambassador at World Institute For Peace
The Office of the Sun does not float twice
BOOK on Rabieh Albouh
BOOK for pearls
World Peace Anthology in Argentina
Anthology of the anthology of six bold birds in Argentina
World Spanish Encyclopedia Flowers

I Want My Poetry to . . .

I want my Poetry to be a sparkle of light
I blow on it and it slips away from my body
Together we smell the first breezes of dawn between rocks and stones
I want my Poetry to
lick our fragile pens
Our fragile thoughts
In a slow charity from night to day
I want it to be a single candle in a single country
Without a leg and an arm
And insulating clothes
Without a wall
I want my poetry
Be words between the mouths of others
I want it to be trees and figs
And air and emptiness
Growing from the mud of the loving
I want it to be an invisible world
And mud or dust or crumbs
From a wooden board
Not inhabited by the ghosts of fire
I want my poetry to
Cities empty of the disease of hatred and loathing
And the abyss of blood in cruelty and death
I want it to be the warmth of childhood in the frost
And the stories of the ancestors and a town of crystal
If it possesses itself, it will fear nothing or soften
Mature for adults
I want my poetry to
Advise the
Above the ancient idols
Flogging the nakedness of the times, a noble lie
I want love in short

I want my poetry to . . . Volume 4

Nandita De nee Chatterjee

Nandita De nee Chatterjee is a Writer/freelance journalist/ Book Editor; ex-Economic Times, published in Statesman, Illustrated Weekly, ET, Telegraph, TOI, Germany Today, VMM, UK, Setu, New York Parrot, Inner Child Press US etc. Co Author in 84 anthologies, 8 Coffee Table Books, Editor of 7 books, 2 journals.

I Want My Poetry to . . .
Intrinsic glory

I want my poetry to
Wash the ground
Where the Lord steps…

To drape the rainbow with a rosy hue
To pour from a nightingale's breast

To glide like a lotus in a pond
Through water murky or pure
When the sun casts its golden glow
Or inky night steals silently in

Like a prayer on a child's lips
I wish my poems are full of hope
Dreams of innocence and wonder
Ceaseless joy and love galore

Like a song of the wind
As it whistles through the maple trees
Soothing the tired doe
Shivering in the white snow

Like an aurora at midnight
Where the sun doesn't rise
Bestowing its brilliance
On the world steeped in umbra deep

A mother's serene smile
As she lulls her baby in her arms
A father's firm clasp
Of a toddler's hands in the park

I want my poetry to
Heal the wounds life inflicts
To speak of peace the world so needs
Discover ways to spread the word

Of happiness waiting at the kerb
Holding hands they must go
Seeking truth, virtue, together
Friend and foe

To speak of the blessings received
An outpour of praise for the grace
Parents, planet, people pledged

Every nightfall we wish and pray
For goodness to come and stay
To seep into our souls deep
To awaken us to glories we seek.

The End

I want my poetry to . . . Volume 4
Kimberly Burnham

A brain health expert (PhD in Integrative Medicine) and award-winning poet, Kimberly Burnham lives with her wife and family in Spokane, Washington. Kim speaks extensively on peace, brain health, and "Awakenings: Peace Dictionary, Language and the Mind, a Daily Brain Health Program." She recently published "Heschel and King Marching to Montgomery A Jewish Guide to Judeo-Tamarian Imagery." Currently work includes "Call and Response To Maya Stein an Anthology of Wild Writing" and a how-to non-fiction book, "Using Ekphrastic Fiction Writing and Poetry to Create Interest and Promote Artists, Writers, and Poets." Follow her at https://amzn.to/4fcWnRB

I Want My Poetry to . . .
The Heart Poetry Build

I Want My Poetry To …
build in me a place from which I can see
vibrant sunsets knowing there are fires burning
and that not everyone is lucky
extending compassion while holding both realities
communicating what is real in me

I Want My Poetry To …
convey my gratitude for shelter, food
above all—love and friendship
I see more clearly when I write poetry
colors, textures, and sounds of life
opening a window for my heart to shine through

I Want My Poetry To …
enable me to percieve the vibrant world in spaces
between contractions, taking actions fueled by the beat
opening the door to the world around me
to see reality: the best of our world

I Want My Poetry To …
bring to life my love of gardens
trees, dogs, and peace sharing
with my neighbors abundance
building a roof over all that is precious
protective while still providing access to
the warmth in a winter's sunset
coolness in green summer shade

I want my poetry to . . . Volume 4
Teodozja Świderska

Teodozja Świderska graduated in Polish philology from University of Opole. Author of five books of poetry. Winner of national poetry competitions. She has published poems in literary magazines and in dozens of anthologies, including international ones. She belongs to Association of Polish Authors in Warsaw (SAP), and Polish Writers' Union.

I Want My Poetry to…

I want my poetry to
be like a water drop for the thirsty
and an island of respite
for those drifting in the ocean of life

May it be a tree from dreams
for exhausted wings
in the tight skies
a reflection from a bird's-eye view
of shaky spans of hope
in the bridge of destiny

I want my poetry to
bring a smile to someone's face
a glazy pearl of emotion
be like a friendly handshake
on the verge of despair and a stone
that knocks off tyrants' crowns

I want ephemeral words of poems
to be like the warmth of bare feet
on oppressed Earth

a human trace of existence

Translated by Anna Maria Stępień

I want my poetry to . . . Volume 4
Anna Maria Stępień

Anna Maria Stępień, economist and English philologist, teaching English and translating for over 2 decades now. She writes poems, short stories, memoirs, anecdotes, both in Polish and English. Translated into almost 40 languages. Editor of multilingual magazines and culture promoter. Member of Literary Society in Mielec.

I Want My Poetry to…

If I only could I would
change the butterflies of wondrous thoughts
into the enchanting rows of words,
into verses magical and sweet.
If I only could I would
praise what one cannot discern
but feels, what flows in veins and tells to live.
The birds would chirp, they would sing
the nicest songs in poems which I would
compose.

If I only could…

A piece of sky for battered hearts,
a voice that some
can't find within themselves
I'd love my poetry to be,
sunny smiles to see
where once the gloom and hope
in the murky prison of dark thoughts.

… a comfy nook for one to hide,
forgetting for a while
the ebbs and flows, the tides,
the storms of life
which carry us to spaces wild where we
have never dreamed to dwell

I want my poetry to... Volume 4
Sujata Paul

Sujata Paul is a Indian trilingual poetess cum author was born in Jadavpur, Kolkata, India. By profession, she is a teacher but writing is her passion. She has authored three books of poems named Whisper of My Soul and Sarang in English and Astitwa in Bengali. Her creative writings are witnessed by the special anthologies like 'Tranquil Muse', 'Spilling Essences',' Vasudha Queen', 'The Spirit of India', 'Sipay', 'Thy Name Is Not Woman', 'Florets of Fancy',' My Tears', 'Petals of Peace', ' Great Women of India' and many more.

I Want My Poetry to . . .
On Greyness

I want my poetry to be the time
When you see me lying in the bed idly
Like a book is leant in the shelf,
Don't get me wrong that the last moment
Is going to be arrived
Having rest doesn't mean one's end.

When you see me sitting calmly under the tree
Staring at the remote paddy field,
Don't try to make me stand
For I am interacting with my soul intimately
That you can't understand.

When you note me composing a poem
And my pen is something away from me
And the diary is relaxing over my lap
Don't try to snatch the things from myself
For I am thinking something higher
To compose a masterpiece.

You don't go to my grey hair
Don't underestimate to see my thin body,
Don't get me wrong for my indifferent eyes
Don't care for my broken health
For they are the harvest of my maturity and greyness as well.

I want my poetry to . . . Volume 4

Kay Salady

Kay Salady is a published poet, photographer, mother, and humanitarian. Her hobbies include cooking, gardening, photographing flowers, and exploring all the Pacific Northwest has to offer. Through her writing, she aspires to touch the lives of others by invoking a sense of joy, hope and comfort.

I Want My Poetry to . . .

Reveal the expressive mind of me
All the while metaphorically
Unveil the lies and hidden truth
Buried deeply since my youth
Evoke emotion and bring to tears
The calloused soul by lending a mirror
To a troubled heart from an honest pen
Showing that feelings are okay and then
Be pressed in gilded books of gold
Be chanted by the young and old
Whisper as from lovers' lips
Seduce with fragrant fingertips
Prove there's hope I know it can
Leave impressions in the sand

I want my poetry to . . . Volume 4
Mark Fleisher

Award-winning writer Mark Fleisher has published six books of poetry and prose. His fifth book – *Knowing When* -- was a finalist for the New Mexico-Arizona Book Co-op and Military Writers Society of America award programs. Based in Albuquerque, New Mexico, he holds a journalism degree from Ohio University and served in the United States Air Force.

I Want My Poetry to . . .

I want my poetry to
beguile you
befuddle you
enlighten you
surprise you
unnerve you
I want my poetry to
touch your brain
touch your soul
touch your heart
make you laugh
make you cry
I want my poetry to
trigger emotions
recall memories
ease your anguish
lighten the darkness
brighten the day
I want my poetry to
be approachable
and draw you in
I want my poetry to
be accessible
and not push you away
If and when at least some
of these "wants"
are accomplished
I shall have done my job

I want my poetry to . . . Volume 4

Md Ejaj Ahamed

Md Ejaj Ahamed (Born: 26 February 1990, Birthplace: Mahendrapur, Aurangabad, Murshidabad, West Bengal, India) is a bilingual poet, writer, editor, journalist, teacher, peace ambassador. His published books are seven and edited books are three. Besides his poems and articles have been published in many joint books and journals. He is the chief editor of Swapner Vela Sahitya Patrika (The Raft of Dreams Literary Magazine).

I Want My Poetry to...

I want my poetry to make a messenger of humanity
Who will protest against injustice and tyranny.

I want my poetry to make a messenger of humanity
Who will spread tranquility.

I want my poetry to make a truth seeker
Who will become also a beauty-maker,
Who always takes beauty by the hand from nature.

I want my poetry to make a painter
Who makes paintings of society and nature with letters.

I want my poetry to make a bridge
Of imagination and deep feelings
My poetry imagines and feels.

I want my poetry to . . . Volume 4
Celia Kurdab Hamadeh

A Lebanese writer, poet and businesswoman who holds a bachelor's degree from American university of Beirut. Author of two books of poetry in the Arabic language in addition to tens of articles on socio-political issues in Lebanon, citizen and women rights and. Her poetry studied by renowned Arab critics. A number of her poems was translated to Italian and Spanish. She writes in English as well. Because of troubled situation In Lebanon, Celia spent long years with her family in KSA then Dubai where she gained extensive work experience in advertising, marketing and PR, and diplomatic translation.

I Want My Poetry to . . .

"I want my poetry to find its way to you "
To Make you wonder with me inside my imagination
And wonder was it me who wrote the words or you.
I want you to dance with me on the banks of words, feeling the joy in you,
Regardless of syllables, rules or rhyme,
Defying distance, place and time.
I don't care if my poems or name remain,
Although in my poems I am "a woman of all times "
A woman your imagination keeps searching for
And you always wonder whom you really adore.
I want my poems to Grow trees and flowers in your way,
Open closed doors to skies you thought impossible to reach,
With no intention to judge or teach.
I want my words to free birds from cages,
Save Trees and animals from the harm of humans,
Embrace free minds and freedom
And to bring joy even when sorrow prevails.
I want my poetry to free the world from wars,
And to Draw a peaceful world to the children of today and tomorrow.
I want my poetry to emanate love
And show you how precious you are,
Regardless of whoever loves you or didn't.
I want women to feel their worth, embrace their mind
And all gifts they got, regardless of looks, color or place
Be independent but yet caring and loving, and above all love who they are,
always worthy of love and respect.
I want my verses to make you love yourself,
And to think twice if you think you aren't enough.
To see beauty in little things even when life gets tough.
I want to draw a green heart on the face of the sky,
For people sometimes don't see
all the greenery around them
Asking for love from the skies
And distracted from seeing heaven's love blooming on earth.
I want my poetry to remain simple, transparent and true,
And for that to be felt by you.
I want my poetry to find its way to you.
What's poetry after all, if it didn't find its way to the light of your eyes!

I want my poetry to... Volume 4
Jill Delbridge

I am ... God's child, Woman, Sunflower amid roses, solitary but, joyful, current season is Autumn. my delicate, yet bold leaves are falling ... time pauses for no one, mindful Winter is coming. bohemian creative, a hope filled dreamer, kin to all human and sentient beings, composition of the universe, rooted deep in femininity, begin and end each day, grateful and humble, student of life for life, daily maintenance of grace, self-love and inner peace, I give my all, or nothing at all. Peace, ONE Love, & Poetry

I Want My Poetry to . . .

inspire you
for a few moments
as you read my humble words
may you find peace
translated in braille
for it is something you can feel
allowing those who feel
they are alone
to know they are not alone
sharing my life, earned wisdom
as a gift from me to you
beyond the loss, hurt, and affliction
there is hope, strength, and resilience
we are the future
all else is history
healing the wounds
of societal curses
uplifting the children in poverty
the forgotten, lost, and lonely
that i too struggle
but nonetheless I persist
Obliterating confines
and invisible division lines
of separateness
for we are ONE
Freedom and respect
for All human beings
and sentient beings
stories to be told
no matter how painful
to be vulnerable yet, heard
Listening without interruption
Motivation for fellow dreamers
to pursue their dreams with vigor
it is never too late to begin
and/ or start over again
don't give up, change up, adapt

I want my poetry to . . . Volume 4

a voice for political prisoners
homeless, ailing, and addicted
keeping ancestors' aspirations alive
Obstacles are stepping stones
laden in wisdom and knowledge
fuel is the pain
use it, bend and twist
within the storms and rain
where there is life
hope is breathing ...
grief and love
are birth from the same seed
fertilize love
and allow love to guide you
scars are survivors' trophies
may my poem
encourage you to be you
and to follow your own
unique life path
Peace, ONE Love, & Poetry!

I want my poetry to . . . Volume 4
Andrew Kouroupos

Andrew Kouroupos, is a writer with works featured in several anthologies. In addition, Andrew's screenplay, *Homeboys*, was showcased at Sundance Film Festival. Most recently, Andrew's short story, *Odee,* was nationally recognized as one of the top 50 short stories of 2024 by Josephson Entertainment + Roadmap Writers.

I Want My Poetry to…

I want my Poetry to speak,
to all the world's injustice though I'm meek,
a Phoenix soaring far above its lair,
a girded bird now brave enough to dare.

I want my Poetry to turn,
the tide of this unjustness so they'll learn,
a forest can be seen despite its trees,
when ruffled by the Phoenix and its breeze.

I want my Poetry to die,
to go where souls are wailing woes of, why,
a Phoenix that descends for martyrs lost,
a voice for those who bravely paid the cost.

I want my Poetry to live,
beyond the years that God to me will give,
a Phoenix penning verses from its dust,
and rising from its grave and rise it must.

I want my poetry to . . . Volume 4
Carthornia Kouroupos

Carthornia Kouroupos is a professor at Rowan College of South Jersey. In addition to being an educator and humanitarian, Carthornia is a published author of five children's books, and a body of poetic works published in several anthologies.

I want my poetry to…

I want my poetry to heal
to help the broken all survive their pain
to give them back the life they cannot feel
to show them that tomorrow's not in vain

I want my poetry to purge
the conscience of the seedy and their gain
ill-gotten with a sordid, selfish urge
and stop another heart from being slain.

I want my poetry to move
a shattered heart to swim before it drowned
and lift it up the mountain that will prove
there's hope beyond their sorrow to be found

I want my poetry to save
to help the broken hearted to forgive
to put them on the road that's past the grave
and piece together love so they can live

I want my poetry to . . . Volume 4

Mutawaf Shaheed

C. E. Shy has been writing since the seventh grade. He continued writing through high school, until he became more involved in sports. After his graduation, he worked at the White Motors Company where he wrote for the company's newspaper. He started a column called: "The Poet's Corner." That was his first published work.

www.innerchildpress.com/c-e-shy.php

I want my poetry to . . . Volume 4

I Want My Poetry to . . . say

Things that you can't say. To open your eyes when necessary. To feel what I felt when I wrote it. To wipe certain sentences on your mind Like I'm sitting right next to you at the time. I want it ask the question , then answer it too. I'd like you to know, that I know just how you feel. If it could have you share these lines sometimes with someone who thinks and feels like you do.

Many times I'm saying me too. I want it turn your head before you turn the corner. To convey the thought that you may need less than you want. For you to find comfort in doing continuous good deeds, even if they are small. My poem should not to let them trick you, don't let them stick you with their sick seeds that produce nothing but rotten fruits

I want it to relax you when you are with me. Sometimes, it could be just dessert or a whole meal. To be a substitute for a narcotic. If you fly with it, then be it so. Want it to help you find what exists between the pillar and the post. I want you to challenge the answer they gave you, that you knew wasn't right.

Making you believe there is a right way to do wrong. I'd like it to take you back the happy moments of your childhood and all that wasn't pleasant leave all of it alone. Since I hardly ever want much, this poem is all I need. Be my guest, please take home.

I want my poetry to... Volume 4
Shareef Abdur Rasheed

Shareef Abdur-Rasheed, AKA Zakir Flo was born and raised in Brooklyn, New York. His education includes Brooklyn College, Suffolk County Community College and Makkah, Saudi Arabia. He is a Veteran of the Viet Nam era, where in 1969 he reverted to his now reverently embraced Islamic Faith. He is very active in the Islamic community and beyond with his teachings, activism and his humanity.

I Want My Poetry to . . .

i want my poetry to
shed light overwhelm
darkness
wake up the sleeping
masses
enhance the status of
the caretakers

i want my poetry to..,

expose the lies of the
leaders
the constant habit of the
bottom feeders

i want my poetry to...,

blossom like gorgeous red roses
have the beauty of composition
like the great composers
enjoin the right forbid the wrong
remind mankind in a beautiful song

i want my poetry to..,

speak on the issues that divide mankind
strike a chord that diminish flaws of the
heart and mind
encourage humanity be humane, kind

i want my poetry to remind

I want my poetry to . . . Volume 4

hülya n. yılmaz

Penn State Professor Emerita, hülya n. yılmaz [sic] is Co-Chair and Director of Editing Services at Inner Child Press International, a published author, and a literary translator. Her poetic work has appeared in numerous anthologies in the U.S.A., and has been presented abroad. She holds a literary excellence award from WIN of B.C.

I Want My Poetry to . . .

seat itself right by you
when you feel weary of the heaviness
life's burdens leave you with in endless abundance

i want my poetry to dab your tears in mid-air
before they set ablaze your worn-out heart
before you submit to the talons of sorrow
before the well of despair entraps you

i want my poetry to hold hands with you
while you tell it your joy-filled memories
while they push your pain and suffering away
while a smile broadens on your childhood-face

 i want my poetry to ease your soul's wailing
as you await it to explode in your silenced voice
as sadness drags you into a breeding ground of nightmares
as they violently shake you out of your nightly sleep

i want my poetry to
     cradle you as if in the arms of a loving mother
          tuck you in while she hums your favorite lullaby
               unbind you from the agony of your adulthood-chains
                    help you to forgive and embrace your self-unforgiving self
                        dispel the vengeful ghosts of your ills of the past
                           chafe away your immense boulder's mass
                              amass for you serene drops of bliss

i want my poetry to
     be a break for you from the harshness of the world
          waft through your dark yesterday into a bright now
               lift your spirit through a breeze that is mate to the mild zephyr
to undiscovered lands as well to the Seven Seas
to the communes on the many luminous moons
to the faraway councils of breath-taking skies
to the cometic homes of ancient curiosities
               in pursuit of the Hindu, the Chinese, the Japanese
                    of the suns of the Egyptians

I want my poetry to... Volume 4

            of the Greek, the Aztec, the African
            of the Navajo, the Inca, the Inuit
            of the Sumerian, the Roman
even though
i do not always
chant "elation!" alone

I want my poetry to . . . Volume 4
William S. Peters, Sr.

A 2016, 2019 and 2025 nominee for the Pulitzer Prize for Literature, William S. Peters, Sr., AKA 'just bill', has devoted himself to poetry since 1966. He holds the passionate conviction that the written word is a necessity, regardless of form. The author's spiritual essence reflects in his socially conscientious actions, all of which serve his efforts to ease his personal angst while contributing to the betterment of humanity and the reconciliation of its plight.

The author says: "I have always likened Life to that of a Garden. So, for me, Life is simply about the Seeds We Sow and Nourish.

I Want My Poetry to . . .

I want my poetry to
Go on and on like
A never ending song
That plays until
The end of eternity

I want my poetry to etch
Unerasable memories
Of joy, peace and love
On the hearts, souls and minds
Of all that hear my voice,
And those who do not as well

I want my poetry to
Help you remember the lyrics
To that divine song,
That everlasting song
That initiated your first heartbeat,
Your first breath,
That song which spawned
Your joy of life,
Your dreams that went beyond
The borders we now
Adhere to, . . .
Those lyrics that whisper
That are ever expanding,
Moment by moment
To help us understand
That 'possibility' is but a word
That limits us
From embracing our
God-Seed,
That small particle of consciousness
That resolves the thorns
Of our existence
And helps us realize
The 'One-ness'
Of all things.

I want my poetry to . . . Volume 4

I want my poetry to evolve
Without cease,
With limitlessness abound
Just as we are destined to do.

I want my poetry
To remind each of us
That we are so much more
Than what the world has told us,
And that our unified truth
Can not be erased
For it,
Like these words scribed
Are immortal
As is poetry

I want my poetry to . . .
Have soul!!!

Epilogue

this is our World . . .
this is our Gift . . .

for our Children !

. . . know that we are the enchanting magicians that nourishes the seeds of dreams and thoughts . . . it is our words that entice the hearts and minds of others to believe there is something grand about the possibilities that life has to offer, and our words tease it forth into action . . . for you are the Writer to whom the Gift of Words has been entrusted . . . wsp

about . . .

Inner Child Press International

Inner Child Press was founded by William S. Peters, Sr., and is a subsidiary of Inner Child Enterprises. We take pride in our writer-oriented vision. Our entire staff is comprised of writers. We fully understand your needs and concerns when it comes to the multiple aspects of the publishing journey. Our areas of specialization includes poetry and prose, and their various sub-genres. When you examine our extensive professional services, all geared toward the authoring-publishing-promotion dynamics, you will find that we have something for every aspiring writer to fit their dreams and their budget.

We offer a full range of services for the writer, including the complete aspects of the writer's publishing interests and other essential services. Browse through our web site to learn more about who we are.

Let us share our Magic with you ...

Other

Meaningful Anthologies

by

Inner Child Press International

Now Available at www.innerchildpress.com

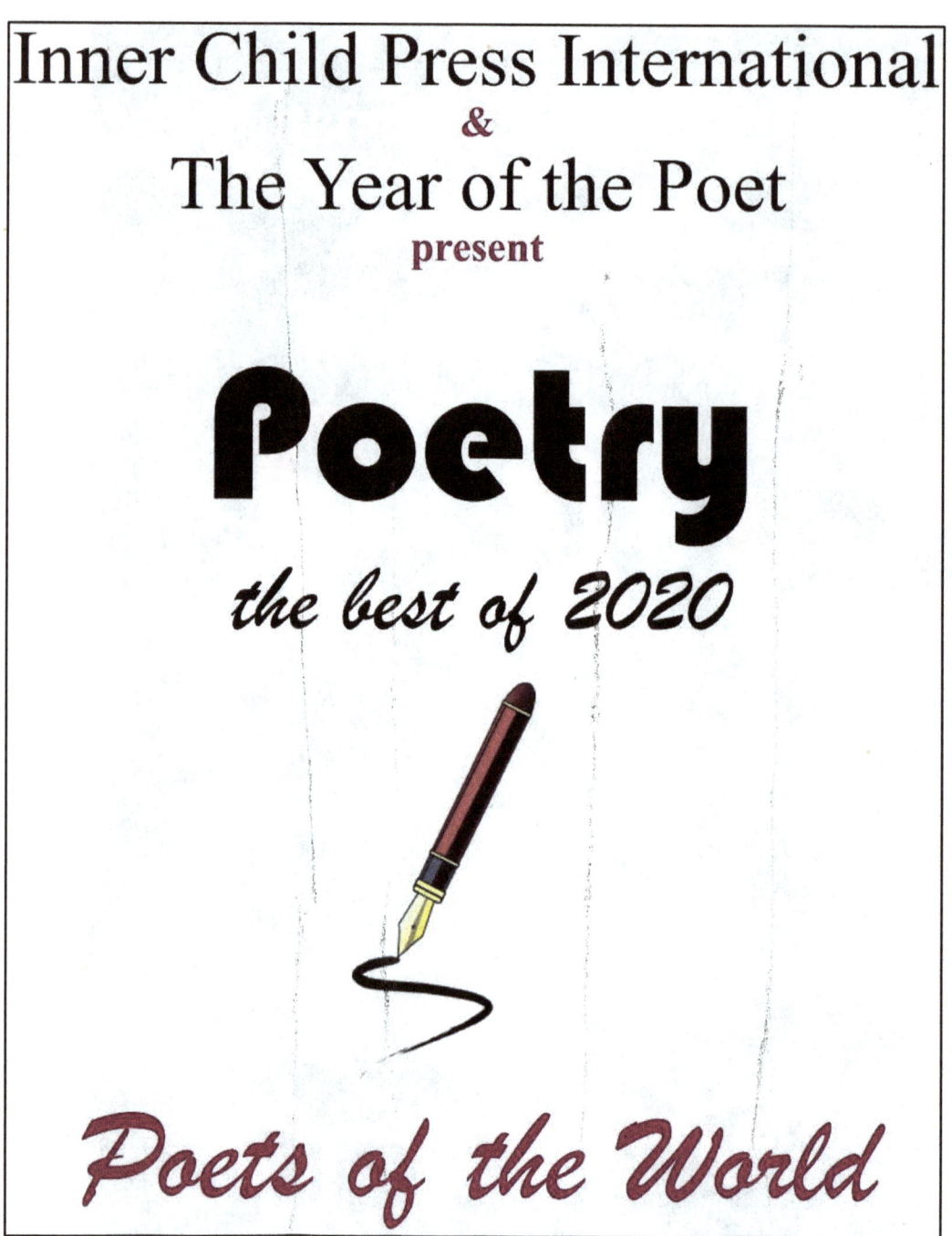

Now Available at www.innerchildpress.com

Now Available at www.innerchildpress.com

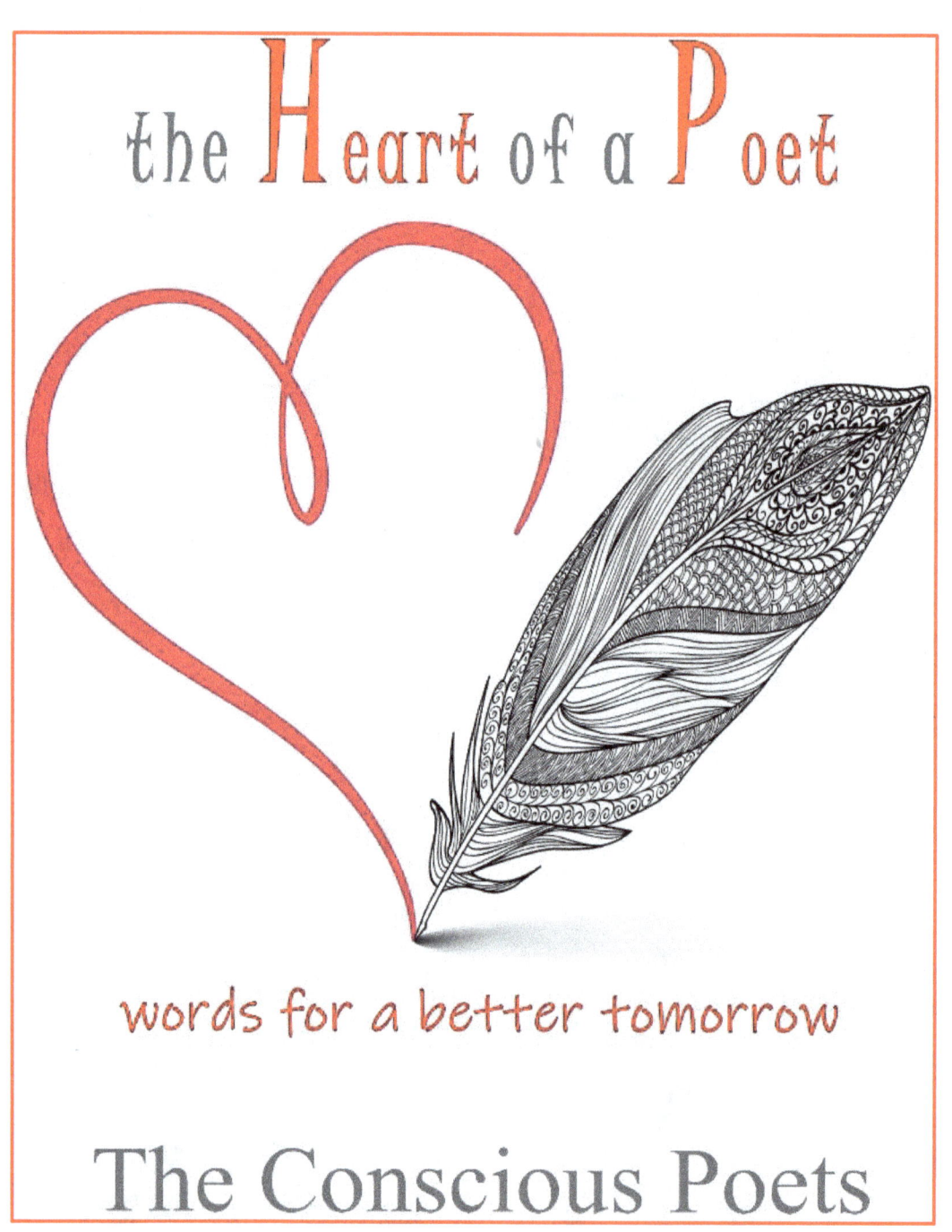

Now Available www.innerchildpress.com

Now Available at www.innerchildpress.com

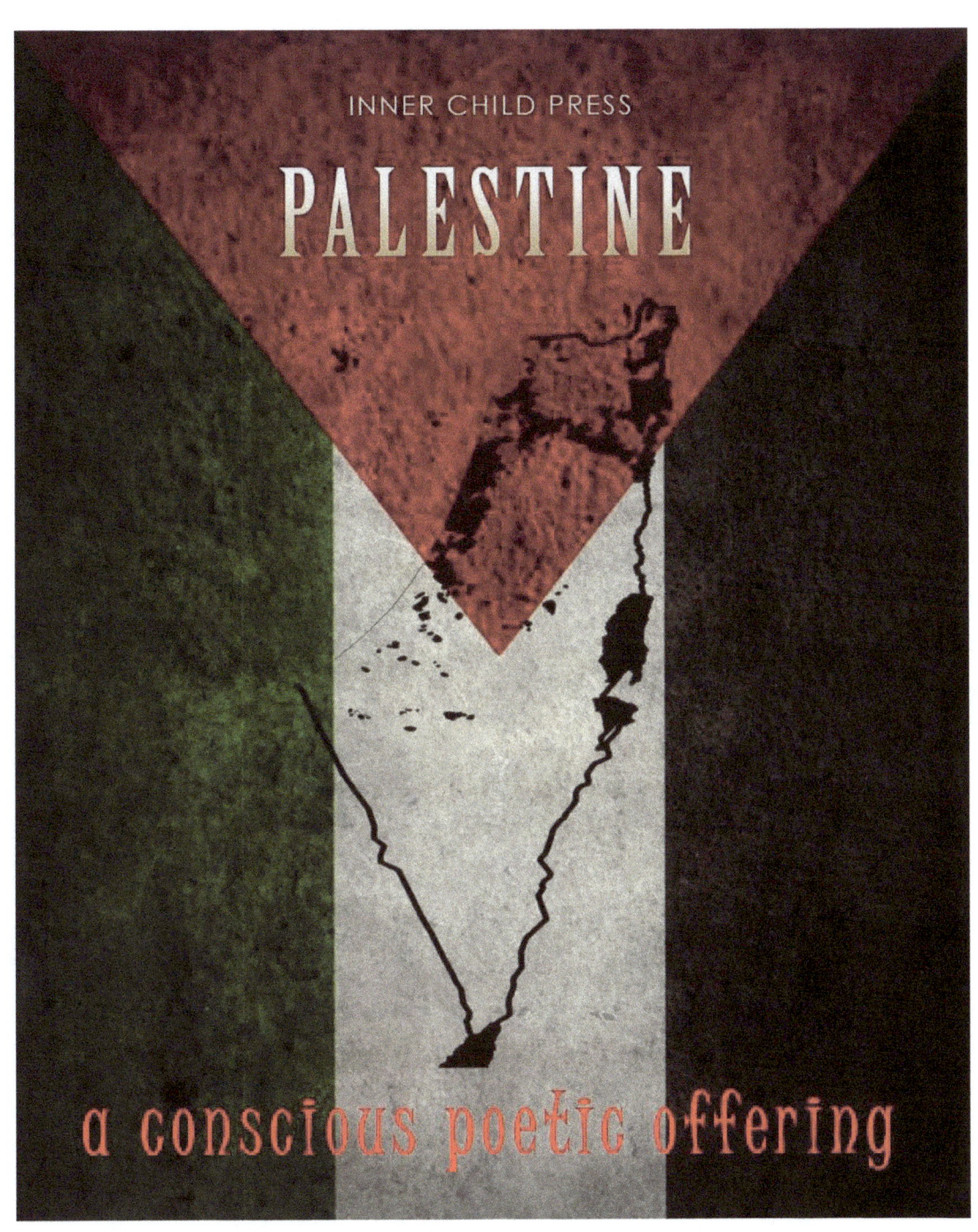

Now Available at www.innerchildpress.com

Now Available at www.innerchildpress.com

Now Available at www.innerchildpress.com

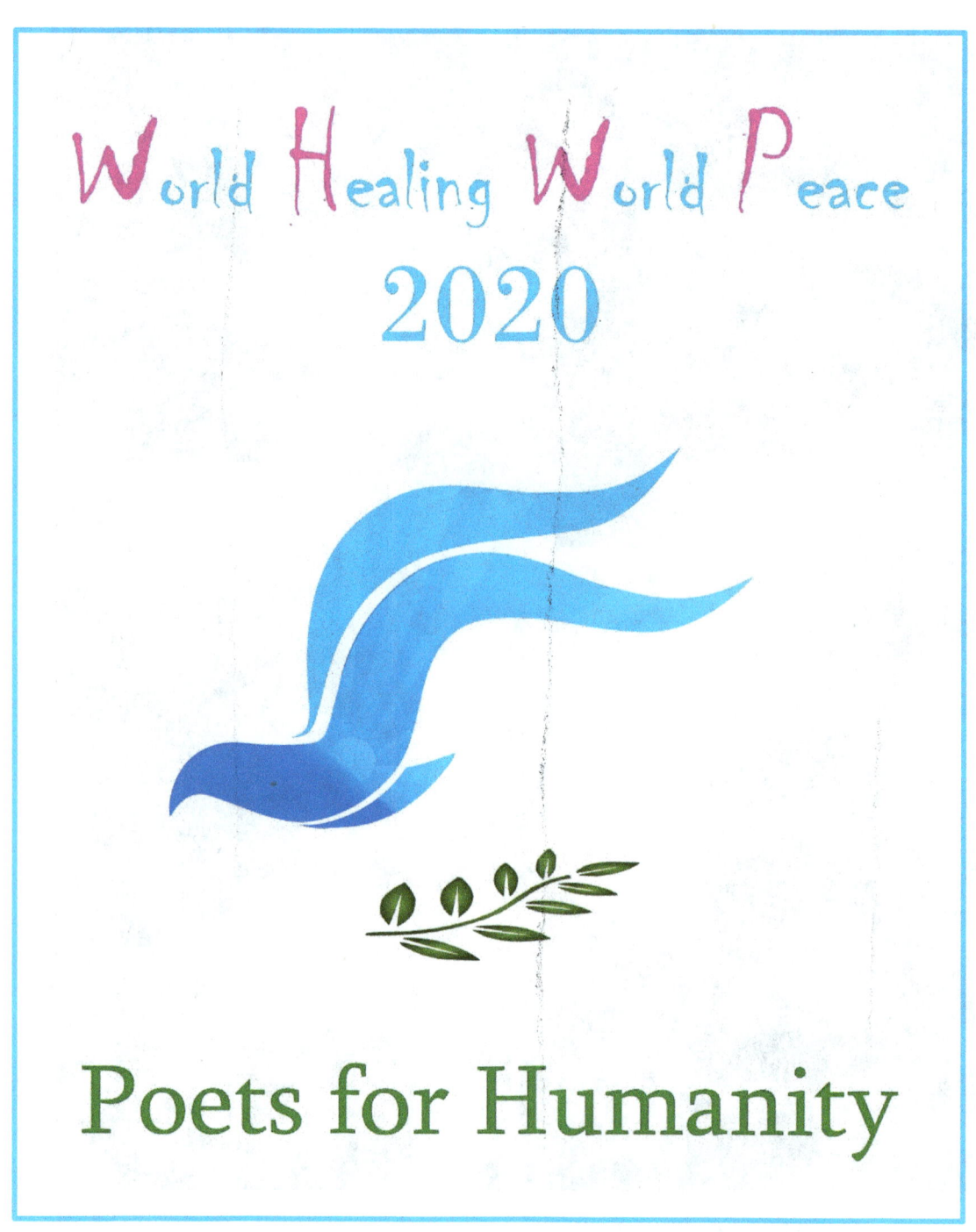

Now Available at www.innerchildpress.com

Now Available at www.innerchildpress.com

Now Available at www.innerchildpress.com

Now Available at www.innerchildpress.com

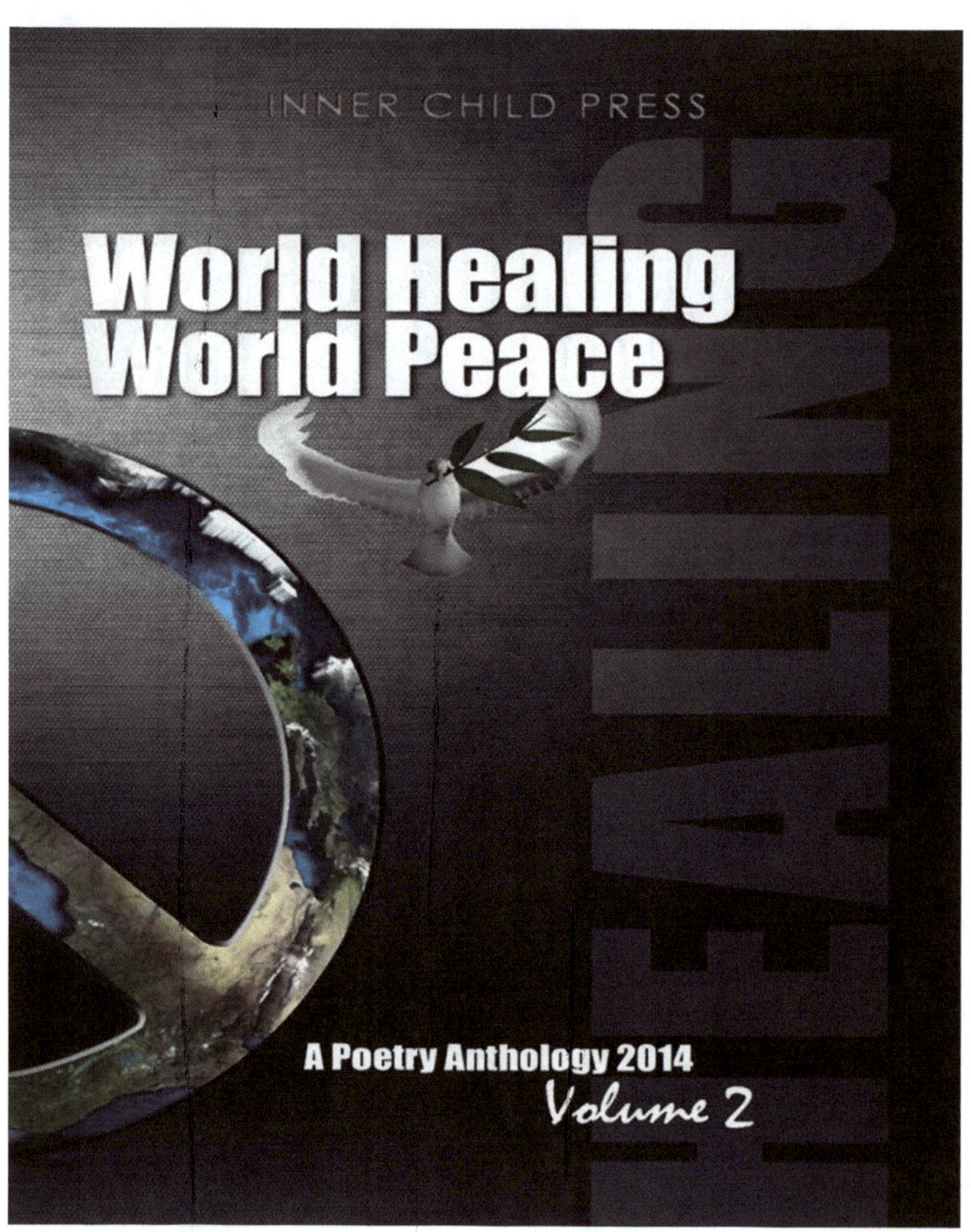

Now Available at www.innerchildpress.com

Now Available at www.innerchildpress.com

Now Available at www.innerchildpress.com

Now Available at www.innerchildpress.com

Now Available at www.innerchildpress.com

Now Available at www.innerchildpress.com

Now Available at www.innerchildpress.com

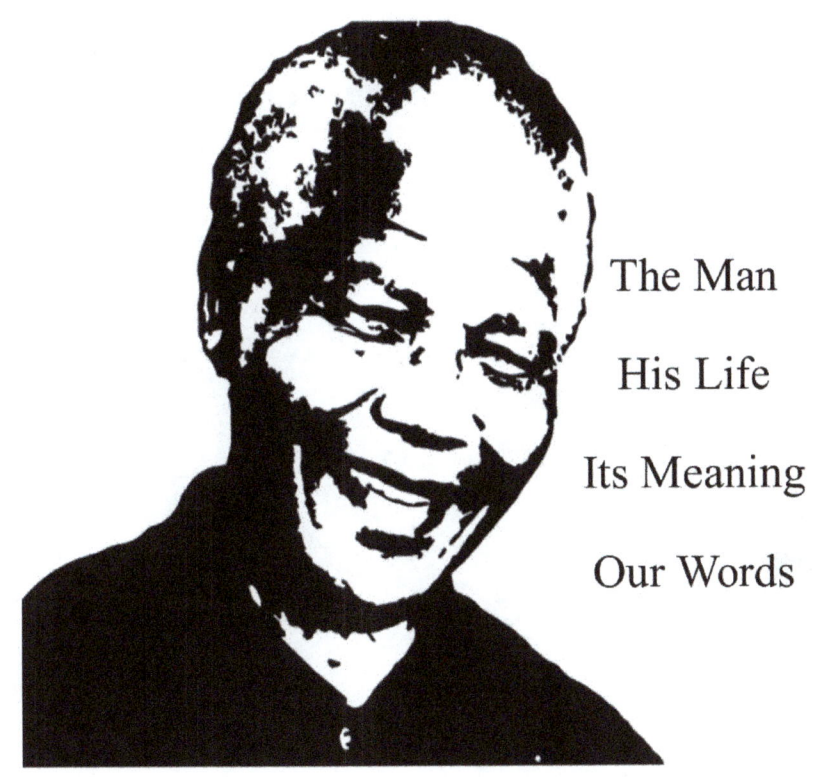

Now Available at www.innerchildpress.com

Now Available at www.innerchildpress.com

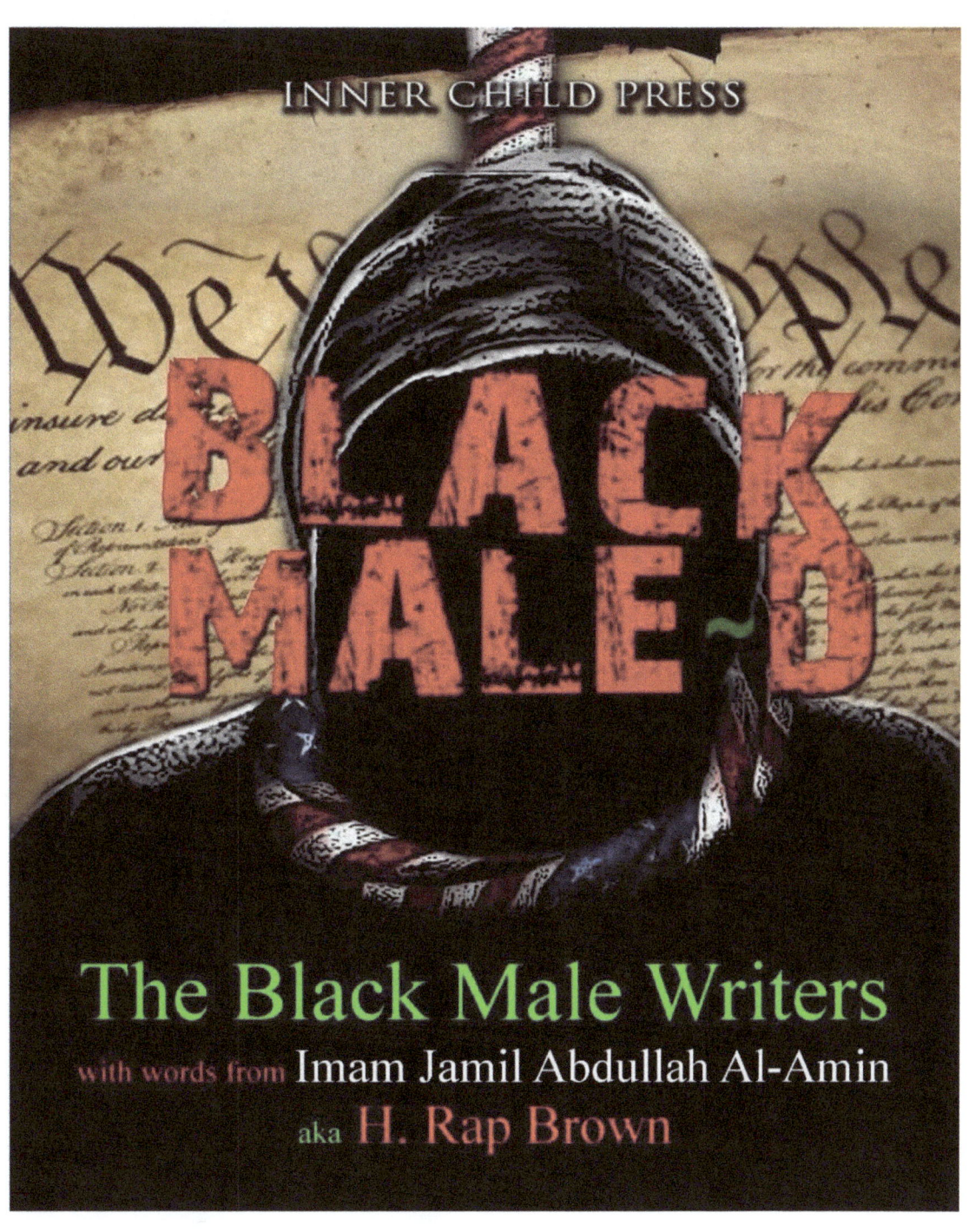

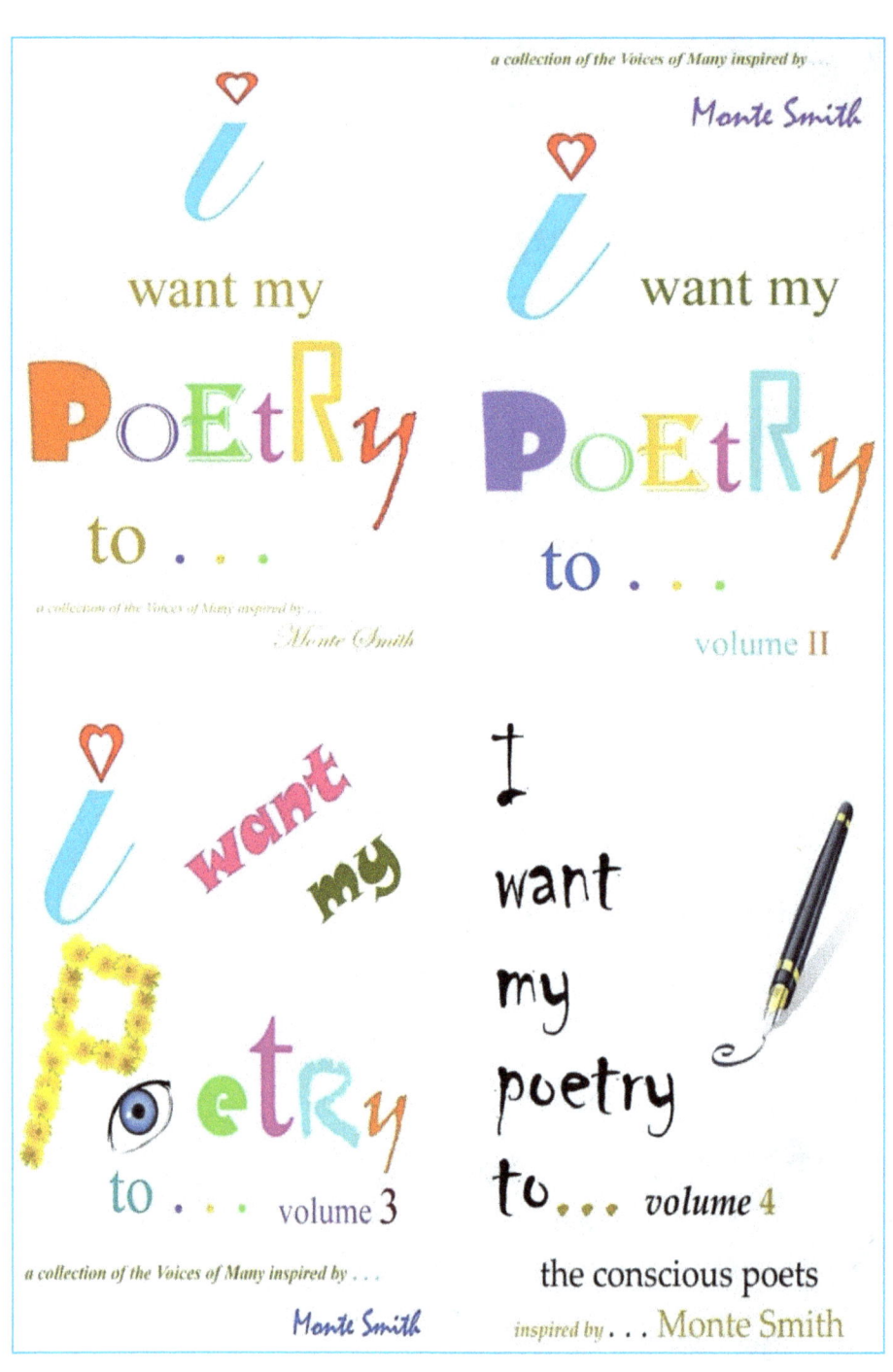

Now Available at www.innerchildpress.com

Now Available at www.innerchildpress.com

Now Available at www.innerchildpress.com

and there is much, much more!

visit . . .

www.innerchildpress.com/anthologies-sales-special.php

Also check out our authors
and all the wonderful books available at:

www.innerchildpress.com/authors-pages

www.worldhealingworldpeacepoerty.com

Inner Child Press International

'building cultural bridges of understanding'

Meet the Board of Directors

William S. Peters, Sr.
Chair Person
Founder
Inner Child Enterprises
Inner Child Press

Hülya N Yılmaz
Director
Editing Services
Co-Chair Person

Nizar Sartawi
Director
International
Relations

Fahredin B. Shehu
Director
Cultural Affairs

Gail Weston Shazor
Director
Anthologies

Kimberly Burnham
Director
Cultural Ambassador
Pacific Northwest
USA

Deborah Smart
Director
Publicity
Marketing

De'Andre Hawthorne
Director
Performance Poetry

Ashok K. Bhargava
Director
WINAwards

www.innerchildpress.com

Inner Child Press International
'building bridges of cultural understanding'
Meet our Cultural Ambassadors

Fahredin Shehu
Director of Cultural
Kosovo

Faleha Hassan
Iraq ~ USA

Elizabeth E. Castillo
Philippines

Antoinette Coleman
Chicago
Midwest USA

Ananda Nepali
Nepal ~ Tibet
Northern India

Kimberly Burnham
Pacific Northwest
USA

Alicja Kuberska
Poland
Eastern Europe

Swapna Behera
India
Southeast Asia

Kolade O. Freedom
Nigeria
West Africa

Monsif Beroual
Morocco
Northern Afric

Ashok K. Bhargava
Canada

Tzemin Ition Tsai
Republic of China
Greater China

Alicia M. Ramírez
Mexico
Central America

Christena AV Williams
Jamaica
Caribbean

Louise Hudon
Eastern Canada

Aziz Mountassir
Morocco
Northern Africa

Shareef Abdur-Rasheed
Southeastern USA

Laure Charazac
France
Western Europe

Mohammad Ikbal Harb
Lebanon
Middle East

Mohamed Abdel Aziz Shmeis
Egypt
Middle East

Hilary Mainga
Kenya
Eastern Africa

Josephus R. Johnson
Liberia

Mennadi Farah
Algeria

Marlon Salem Gruezo
Philippines

Khalice Jade
Algeria
France

www.innerchildpress.com

Advisory Board

World Healing, World Peace Foundation
human beings for humanity

2025

worldhealingworldpeacefoundation.org

Inner Child Press International

Inner Child Press International is a publishing company founded and operated by writers. Our personal publishing experiences provide us an intimate understanding of the sometimes-daunting challenges writers, new and seasoned, may face in the business of publishing and marketing their creative "Written Work".

For more Information:

Inner Child Press International

www.innerchildpress.com

intouch@innerchildpress.com

www.ingramcontent.com/pod-product-compliance
Lightning Source LLC
Chambersburg PA
CBHW081836170426
43199CB00017B/2749